Insurance Law

by
Margaret C. Jasper

Oceana's Legal Almanac Series:
Law for the Layperson

1998
Oceana Publications, Inc.
Dobbs Ferry, N.Y.

Information contained in this work has been obtained by Oceana Publications from sources believed to be reliable. However, neither the Publisher nor its authors guarantee the accuracy or completeness of any information published herein, and neither Oceana nor its authors shall be responsible for any errors, omissions or damages arising from the use of this information. This work is published with the understanding that Oceana and its authors are supplying information, but are not attempting to render legal or other professional services. If such services are required, the assistance of an appropriate professional should be sought.

Library of Congress Cataloging-in-Publication Data

Jasper, Margaret C.
Insurance law / by Margaret C. Jasper.
p. cm.— (Oceana's legal almanac series. Law for the layperson)
ISBN 0-379-11330-9 (alk. paper)
1. Insurance law—United States—Popular works. 2. Insurance—United States—Popular works. I. Title. II. Series.
KF1164.6.J37 1998 98-45141
346.73'086—dc21 CIP

Oceana's Legal Almanac Series: Law for the Layperson
ISSN: 1075-7376

Manufactured in the United States of America on acid-free paper.

To My Husband Chris

Your love and support
are my motivation and inspiration

-and-

In memory of my son, Jimmy

ABOUT THE AUTHOR

MARGARET C. JASPER is an attorney engaged in the general practice of law in South Salem, New York, concentrating in the areas of personal injury and entertainment law. Ms. Jasper holds a Juris Doctor degree from Pace University School of Law, White Plains, New York, is a member of the New York and Connecticut bars, and is certified to practice before the United States District Courts for the Southern and Eastern Districts of New York, and the United States Supreme Court.

Ms. Jasper has been appointed to the panel of arbitrators of the American Arbitration Association and the law guardian panel for the Family Court of the State of New York, is a member of the Association of Trial Lawyers of America, and is a New York State licensed real estate broker and member of the Westchester County Board of Realtors, operating as Jasper Real Estate, in South Salem, New York.

Ms. Jasper is the author and general editor of the following legal almanacs: Juvenile Justice and Children's Law; Marriage and Divorce; Estate Planning; The Law of Contracts; The Law of Dispute Resolution; Law for the Small Business Owner; The Law of Personal Injury; Real Estate Law for the Homeowner and Broker; Everyday Legal Forms; Dictionary of Selected Legal Terms; The Law of Medical Malpractice; The Law of Product Liability; The Law of No-Fault Insurance; The Law of Immigration; The Law of Libel and Slander; The Law of Buying and Selling; Elder Law; The Right to Die; AIDS Law; The Law of Obscenity and Pornography; The Law of Child Custody; The Law of Debt Collection; Consumer Rights Law; Bankruptcy Law for the Individual Debtor; Victim's Rights Law; Animal Rights Law; Workers' Compensation Law; Employee Rights in theWorkplace; Probate Law; Environmental Law; Labor Law; The Americans with Disabilities Act; The Law of Capital Punishment; Education Law; The Law of Violence Against Women; and Landlord-Tenant Law.

TABLE OF CONTENTS

INTRODUCTION

Insurance law deals with issues that affect almost every individual in some manner, at some time in their life. This almanac discusses the major aspects of insurance law to provide the reader with a basic understanding of insurance principles and practices, and to assist the consumer in making informed decisions about their insurance needs. The nature of insurance, its regulation, and the most common types of insurance coverage are explored.

The Appendices provide resource directories, relevant statutes, sample documents; and other pertinent information and data. The Glossary contains definitions of many of the terms used throughout the almanac.

CHAPTER 1:

AN OVERVIEW

The Nature of Insurance

Insurance is generally defined as a contract whereby one party, in return for compensation, undertakes to indemnify another party against loss, damages, or liability arising from some contingent or unknown event. The party undertaking the risk is known as the "insurer" or "underwriter." The party who pays for this protection is known as the "insured."

The monies paid by the insured—called "premiums"—are collected from all of the insureds and placed into a general fund from which payments are made to an insured who suffers a covered loss as set forth in the contract. Insurance is generally classified according to the nature of the risk involved. Common types of insurance cover life, health, property and liability.

Thus, each insured contributes to some degree for the losses of all of the other insureds. While one insured may never recoup the amount of money paid into the fund, others may be compensated many times over what they have contributed. But that is the nature of insurance—a gamble against the odds.

To this end, the insurer is responsible for calculating premiums that will cover projected losses as well as the administrative and related costs of running the insurance company. The insurer must take into account the number of insureds, the likelihood that the specified losses will occur, and the probable dollar amount of the losses should they occur.

The Risk of Loss

Absent insurance, the risk of most losses are usually borne by the individual. A person without health insurance is required to pay their own medical expenses. An individual without homeowner's insurance would have to provide their own funds to rebuild their home if it is destroyed by fire.

Another may be responsible for bearing some or all of an individual's losses under certain situations, or under certain statutes. For example, a worker injured on the job is usually compensated under the applicable workers' compensation statutes. In addition, if someone is responsible for causing another's loss—intentionally or negligently—that individual, or his or her insurer, would be responsible for the other's loss.

Insurance Industry Regulation

In 1868, the United States Supreme Court determined in *Paul v. Virginia*, 75 U.S. 168 (1868), that authority to regulate the insurance industry should be left to the individual states, reasoning that insurance contracts were local in nature, and did not affect interstate commerce.

This ruling was reversed in *United States v. South-Eastern Underwriters Association*, 322 U.S. 533 (1944), wherein the Supreme Court held that insurance transactions did affect interstate commerce because, although the contract may be local in nature, the insurance business itself is conducted across state lines, thus implicating the Commerce Clause.

This reversal—in large part due to the expansion of federal powers during the eighty interim years following the *Paul* decision—exposed the insurance industry to federal regulation. Nevertheless, Congress did not intervene and continued to entrust the regulation of the insurance industry to the states by enacting the *McCarran-Ferguson Act* in 1945 which states:

> Congress hereby declares that the continued regulation and taxation by the several States of the business of insurance is in the public interest, and that silence on the part of Congress shall not be construed to impose any barrier to the regulation or taxation of such business by the several States.

Nevertheless, the federal government did retain the right to regulate insurance in cases where (i) a particular state fails to sufficiently regulate a specific activity; or (ii) Congress expressly overrides a state law; or (iii) a state regulation violates the U.S. Constitution.

Thus, availability, provisions, and insurance rates—e.g., for automobile, home and life insurance—are normally set on a state-by-state basis. For example, earthquake and flood insurance may be available in some states and not others, and no-fault automobile insurance is not mandatory in all states. In addition, the cost of identical insurance coverage varies greatly among the states.

CHAPTER 2:

LIFE INSURANCE

In General

A life insurance policy is basically a contract between an individual and an insurance company that provides for the payment of a specified sum of money to the beneficiary named in the policy upon the death of the insured. The insurable interest is the life of the insured. The policy is generally purchased in order to minimize the financial impact of the insured's death on his or her beneficiaries, who are usually the insured's spouse and children. This chapter attempts to give the reader a general understanding of the various types of life insurance products available on the market, and the coverage they afford the consumer.

There are two basic types of life insurance policies: (i) the term policy; and (ii) the cash value policy.

Term Life Insurance Policy

A term life insurance policy covers the insured for a specified term of one or more years in return for an annual premium. The annual premium may escalate in accordance with one's life expectancy. Death benefits are only paid if the insured dies within the specified term. Some term policies are renewable. However, each time the policy is renewed, the premium increases.

There is no cash value to a term insurance policy during the life of the insured. The policy merely provides a cash benefit to the designated beneficiary upon the insured's death. Some term insurance policies are "convertible," which means that the term policy can be traded for a whole life policy during the conversion period. However, higher premiums will be charged for the new policy.

Cash Value Life Insurance Policy

Unlike the term policy, the cash value life insurance policy usually charges an annual premium that remains the same each year. Cash value policies, while generally more expensive than term policies, offer an additional financial incentive because a portion of the premium is invested and has cash value during the life of the insured. The cash value of the policy may be used to offset premium payments.

In addition, the policyholder may be able to borrow money against the cash value of the policy, which acts as collateral for the loan. The life insurance company generally designates a rate of interest in the policy. However, if the insured dies while a loan is outstanding against the policy, that amount will be deducted from the death benefits. Also, if the insured stops paying the premiums, any outstanding loan amount would be deducted from the cash value payable.

There are also tax benefits to cash value policies in that earnings generated by the policy are generally not taxed while the policy remains in force. If the policyholder decides to stop paying the premiums, he or she can take the specified cash value, also known as the "nonforfeiture benefits" of the policy.

Whole Life Insurance Policy

The most common type of cash value policy is the whole life insurance policy. A whole life policy gives the insured death benefit protection during his or her entire life. The most common whole life policy is known as "straight life" insurance. The same premium is paid for this insurance for as long as the insured lives. Although the premiums for a straight life policy are usually much higher than initial term insurance premiums, in the long run, this type of policy may prove less costly than the term insurance policy, which would become increasingly expensive with each successive renewal.

Another type of whole life policy is one under which the premiums are paid for a specified number of years in return for life-long protection. The premiums for this type of policy, however, are much higher.

Alternative Life Insurance Products

Life insurance policies offering different types of coverage have emerged to give consumers a broader range of choices. As further discussed below, two insurance products growing in popularity are: (i) universal life insurance; and (ii) variable life insurance. Although these policies do not provide the guarantees contained in the more traditional policies, the rate of return may be higher because it is contingent upon the performance of invested premiums.

Universal Life Insurance

Universal life insurance coverage gives policyholders many of the same benefits as whole life policies offer—e.g., cash value and control over premium payments and the amount of death benefit payable—however, they are generally less expensive than whole life coverage. The downside is that the cash value is not guaranteed as it is with the whole life policy, but depends on the performance of invested premium funds.

Variable Life Insurance

Variable life insurance coverage contains many of the same features as universal life coverage, however, the premiums and death benefits are more directly linked to the performance of investments, and policyholders have more control over the manner in which their funds are invested. Therefore, sellers of variable life insurance products are subject to registration with the United States Securities & Exchange Commission.

Purchasing Life Insurance

Purchasing life insurance is essential when planning for the financial future of one's family. It is important to seek professional advice from a qualified insurance representative in order to determine how much life insurance one should purchase in order to meet the needs of surviving loved ones upon the insured's death. Of course, one must also consider the cost of purchasing the right amount of insurance coverage that fits within one's budget. It is also important to be aware of mortality rates when evaluating insurance needs.

A table setting forth the average life expectancy for Americans as of 1996, as prepared by the U.S. Department of Health National Center for Health Statistics, is set forth at Appendix 1.

One basic way to determine how much life insurance to purchase is to first figure out how much income the insured's family would need if he or she died. A rough estimate can be determined by calculating a monthly budget, which should include the following:

Home mortgage, taxes, and insurance;

Household repairs and upkeep;

Utilities;

Food and clothing;

Medical and dental expenses;

Automobile payment, repairs, insurance, and upkeep; and

Miscellaneous expenses.

One should also take into consideration any other income the family will have that may supplement the life insurance income, such as additional earnings, social security income, pension income, or other benefits.

A table listing the average life insurance coverage maintained per household, categorized by state, is set forth at Appendix 2.

When shopping for insurance, it is important to research the track record of the insurance company you purchase your policy from, and make sure the company is in stable financial condition.

A list of the fifty top-rated life and health insurance companies is set forth at Appendix 3.

Minor Beneficiaries

When minor children are named as beneficiaries of a life insurance policy, the proceeds must be overseen by an adult guardian until the minor reaches the legal age of majority. It is imperative that the insured provide for the selection of a guardian to avoid the need for court appointment. There are several ways to designate a guardian.

For example, a guardian of the proceeds can be named in the insured's will. Alternatively, instead of naming a minor as a beneficiary, an adult beneficiary can be named, who will manage the minor's funds until he or she reaches adulthood. However, it is critical that one make sure the adult beneficiary will follow the insured's wishes, and use the money for the benefit of the child. Thus, the adult beneficiary is generally the insured's spouse, a trusted relative, or close friend.

One can also provide for minor children by designating a "living trust" as the beneficiary of the policy, and the children as beneficiaries of that trust. A living trust has the advantages of allowing the insured to provide for the manner in which the proceeds will be used for the children, and also allows the insured to continue the trust until an age deemed appropriate for the child to manage his or her own affairs.

Insurance Proceeds

Insurance proceeds are not subject to the provisions of the deceased's will, nor to the rules of inheritance, thereby avoiding the probate process. Therefore, the proceeds are not part of the deceased's estate, and go directly to the named beneficiary upon the insured's death, with little cost or delay.

However, if the insured names the estate as beneficiary, the proceeds will be paid to the estate. When the named beneficiary is the estate, a lump sum cash payment is usually made by the insurance company and can be used to cover the immediate expenses of the estate without having to resort to the quick and often unprofitable sale of non-liquid assets, such as real estate. It is important to avoid the need for such tactics because when the real estate market is down, the property may have to be sold at a loss.

When the named beneficiary is an individual, there are usually several payout options available at the election of the insured and, sometimes, the beneficiary. For example, the insured may elect to have the proceeds paid out in installments over a specified period of time, with interest. In that case, the interest on the principal is taxable income to the recipient. In the alternative, the insured may elect to have the proceeds applied to the purchase of an annuity to be paid out over the lifetime of the beneficiary. This is particularly useful in the case of a handicapped child who will need lifelong care. Annuities are further discussed below.

Again, it is important to determine what the needs of the surviving family will be upon one's death in order to determine the best payout option. It may be that the family will need more money in the years immediately following the insured's death, in order to make the necessary adjustment to the sudden loss of income, particularly if the insured is the breadwinner of the family, and if there are minor children still in need of support and further education.

Tax Considerations

Although the proceeds from a life insurance policy are normally not subject to income tax, they may be subject to estate tax, depending on the size of the deceased's estate. Currently, an estate must be worth $600,000 or more to be subject to federal estate taxation. Thus, in order for the estate to incur federal estate taxes, the net value of the estate plus the amount of the life insurance proceeds must total at least $600,000.

Transferring Ownership of the Policy

One way to avoid or reduce federal estate taxes if one's estate is large enough to incur such taxes is to transfer ownership of the life insurance policy. If someone other than the insured owns the policy at the time of the insured's death, the proceeds are not included in the deceased's federal taxable estate.

A sample form for the transfer of ownership of a life insurance policy is set forth at Appendix 4.

The owner of a life insurance policy has the right to transfer ownership of the policy to any third party, including the beneficiary. Once ownership of the policy is transferred, however, the insured loses all control over the policy—i.e., the insured can no longer change the named beneficiary of the policy or cancel the policy. Thus, if one spouse transfers ownership of a policy to the other spouse, that spouse continues to own the policy even if there is a subsequent divorce.

There are certain Internal Revenue Service (IRS) rules that can undermine transfer of ownership in some cases. For example, if the insured dies within three years of the transfer, the IRS will disallow the transfer for the purposes of federal estate taxation. Therefore, if one intends to transfer ownership of a life insurance policy, it should be done as early as possible. In addition, if the insured retains any ownership rights or control over the policy— i.e., the "incidents of ownership"—the IRS will include the proceeds of the policy in the deceased's taxable estate. This could result, for example, if one transfers the policy to another, but retains the legal right to perform various acts, such as changing the beneficiaries, canceling the policy, or paying the premiums.

The transfer of a life insurance policy will be considered a gift by the IRS or other taxing authorities, except in the unusual case where the transferee actually pays for the policy. Consequently, transfer of a policy would result in the assessment of a gift tax in an amount determined based on the current value of the policy. Fortunately, however, this tax would be less than the tax assessed if the policy is left in the estate, since the value of the policy during the life of an insured is much less than the proceeds payable under the policy upon the insured's death.

Transferring Ownership to a Trust

Another way to avoid or reduce estate taxes is for the insured to transfer ownership of his or her life insurance policy to a trust, known as an "irrevocable life insurance trust." When an irrevocable life insurance trust is established as a legal entity, the trust becomes the new owner of the policy. Certain requirements govern life insurance trusts. For example, the trust must be irrevocable. If the insured retains any rights to revoke the trust, he or she can be considered the owner of the policy and the proceeds will be included in the taxable estate upon his or her death. In addition, as with the transfer of ownership of a life insurance policy, one cannot be the trustee of the trust. Further, the trust must be established at least three years prior to the insured's death.

The advantage of naming a trust as the new owner of a life insurance policy is that it avoids some of the risks involved when an individual is named as the owner. For example, since the trust can be instructed to keep the life insurance policy in effect until the insured dies, he or she need not worry that the new owner will fail to pay the premiums, or decide to cash in the policy while the insured is still alive.

Need for Periodic Review of the Policy

It is important to review one's life insurance policies on a regular basis, particularly if there has been a change in the insured's status, such as a divorce or marriage. One should make sure that the person or persons named as beneficiaries in the policy are those whom the insured wants the insurance proceeds to go to at the time of his or her death. Therefore, one should review and update the named beneficiaries on a regular basis to make sure they are properly designated. One should also periodically review the size of one's estate, including the insurance policy proceeds, to most effectively plan for and reduce the estimated estate taxes, if any.

Annuities

The term "annuity" basically refers to a contract between an individual and a financial institution—usually a life insurance company—whereby the insurer, in return for an advance payment of a sum of money, agrees to make periodic payments to the individual for a specified period of time. The specific terms of the annuity are governed by the contract between the individual and the life insurance company. Generally, there is no limit on the amount of funds which can be paid into an annuity contract.

Although annuities have been classified as a type of life insurance, they generally serve a number of other purposes. As discussed above, life insurance is generally purchased to provide security in case of premature death. Annuities, unlike life insurance, basically provide the purchaser security in case of an extended lifespan, and are typically purchased in order to accumulate and protect one's wealth.

Many individuals purchase annuities in order to provide for their retirement, and to make sure that they are financially prepared in case of catastrophe or long-term illness. Others wish to use annuities in order to accumulate wealth to pass on to their heirs while taking advantage of certain tax benefits that annuities provide.

Like life insurance proceeds, an annuity contract passes to the beneficiaries outside of the will, and thus is not subject to probate. The beneficiary of the annuity has the option of keeping the contract in force, thus continuing to defer taxes on the earnings. The policyholder is usually guaranteed a death benefit equal to the greater of the face amount or the market value of the annuity contract.

Fixed Annuities

A "fixed" annuity generally refers to an annuity policy under which the policyholder makes a lump sum payment or series of payments, into an annuity product. Under this traditional type of annuity contract, the named beneficiary is generally entitled to receive a series of annuity payments, which are "fixed" in advance in terms of the amount of payment, the frequency of the distribution, and the duration that such payments will be made.

Dissatisfaction with the low interest rates accompanying fixed annuity products led to a number of alternative investment instruments which yield a more variable return, such as variable annuities and other insurance products. Nevertheless, unlike a fixed annuity, the performance risk of these investments rests with the policyholder and not the insurance company.

Variable Annuities

Variable annuities are more flexible, permitting the owner to take advantage of the favorable taxation of annuities, while also allowing for investment of the annuity payments in a broad range of products. Although this is similar to investment in mutual funds, the variable annuities offer death benefit provisions, and provide insurance that the owner will always be entitled to the face amount of the annuity contract, regardless of the performance of its investments. In addition, although annual fees may be higher for variable annuities, they do not require the up-front fees generally required of mutual funds. Nevertheless, there may be significant withdrawal penalties.

Annuitization

Under the annuity contract, the policyholder may elect to receive guaranteed periodic payments over the policyholder's life, which upon death also continue to be paid to the beneficiary during their lifetime. This is known as "annuitization." A married couple may elect this type of coverage to ensure that the surviving spouse is taken care of following the death of the other spouse. One drawback to annuitization is that once the policyholder and the beneficiary die, the contract ceases to exist and the remaining assets, if any, revert to the insurance company.

An alternative type of annuity contract offering similar protection is a "period certain annuitization" policy under which the policyholder can elect to receive payments for the greater of a guaranteed minimum number of years, or the policyholder's lifetime. For example, if the guaranteed minimum were 15 years, and the policyholder died after 5 years, the beneficiary would receive payments for the remaining 10 years. Alternatively, if the policyholder lived for 25 more years, he or she would receive payments during all 25 years.

In addition, many annuity contracts include "step-up" provisions, which increase the amount of the guaranteed benefit at set intervals, e.g., 5 or 10 years.

Taxation and Penalties

One major benefit of the annuity contract is its minimization of taxation. The annuity contract earnings are exempt from all taxes while the contract is in effect. The owner of the annuity decides when funds will be paid out on the contract. Although disbursements from the account are then subject to taxation, the earnings do not affect social security income.

Annuitization, as discussed above, receives more favorable tax treatment than withdrawing funds from an annuity contract. Annuity payments are generally only taxed at one-half the rate of fund withdrawals. The Internal Revenue Service considers annuity payments to be made up of both earnings and return of the original investment, whereas withdrawals are considered to be earnings which are taxable at ordinary income tax rates.

As with many types of retirement accounts, early withdrawal of annuity funds are subject to penalty. However, funds can remain in the account indefinitely without penalty.

Annuities as Settlements in Lawsuits

Annuities are also often used in settling lawsuits. In a negligence case, where a plaintiff's damages are considerable, a defendant may agree to purchase an annuity contract which would compensate the plaintiff over a specified period of time, rather than pay the present dollar value of such a contract.

This is possible because the insurer receives a lump sum of money when the defendant purchases the annuity. That money is then invested and earns interest from which the insurer can afford to pay the plaintiff more than the initial sum of money invested, and still make a profit.

A list of the forty top-rated annuity companies is set forth at Appendix 5.

CHAPTER 3:

HEALTH INSURANCE

Private Health Insurance

Private health insurance is a type of insurance employees may obtain as a benefit of their employment. The employer is generally responsible for paying all or most of the premium payments. Although the employee is usually entitled to choose the type of plan, the employer is entitled to choose the coverage options.

Individuals who work for employers who do not offer health insurance benefits, or who are self-employed, can purchase coverage on their own at generally higher rates. Sometimes unions and professional associations offer their members group rates for health insurance.

Types of Private Health Insurance

Private health insurance plans generally fall under the categories of either (i) traditional health insurance; or (ii) managed care.

Traditional Health Insurance

Traditional health insurance plans—commonly referred to as "fee-for-service" plans—are basically indemnification policies. Under a fee-for-service plan, the insured generally pays a yearly deductible up-front, after which the insurance carrier picks up all or most of the remaining medical expenses for the year.

Under the fee-for-service plan, the insured retains control over choosing their own medical providers, including specialists, without the need for obtaining referrals from a primary physician. The insurance carrier is generally not involved in determining the necessity of the medical treatment.

The disadvantages of fee-for-service plans is that they require the insured to pay more out-of-pocket costs, such as the deductible. In addition, most insurance carriers only pay up to 80% of the remaining medical expenses, leaving the insured responsible for the difference. However, most insurance carriers pay 100% of out-of-pocket expenses once the insured's medical bills reach a specified amount, which is generally quite high.

If the medical provider is one who requires immediate payment, the insured may have to pay the entire bill at the time service is rendered, and then submit it to the carrier for payment of the covered amount.

In addition, insurance carriers generally refer to a chart of "reasonable and customary" medical costs, which is based on the average amount charged for similar services by other medical providers in the area. If the medical provider is one who does not adhere to such a chart, he or she may also seek the difference from the insured.

Managed Care

The majority of private health insurance coverage available today contains some type of managed care plan. Managed care plans generally involve an agreement between an insurance carrier and a selected network of health care providers. There are significant financial incentives offered to the insured if they use the selected providers according to the type of plan and the procedure set forth under the specific plan.

The four basic types of managed health care plans include the: (i) Health Maintenance Organization (HMO); (ii) Preferred Provider Organizations (PPO); (iii) Exclusive Provider Organization (EPO); and (iii) Point-of-Service Plan (POS)

Health Maintenance Organization (HMO)

A Health Maintenance Organization is generally the least flexible type of managed care health plan. Under this plan, the insured is required to visit only those medical providers within the HMO plan. The HMO may be located in a central medical facility where all of the plan medical providers operate, or may consist of a network of individual offices.

Under an HMO plan, the insured must obtain permission from their assigned primary care physician before seeking medical care from a specialist. Further, if the insured seeks medical treatment from medical providers outside of the plan, he or she must generally bear the expense without reimbursement.

The advantage of an HMO plan is that the co-payment, if any, is very small, and the premiums are very low. In addition, the HMO generally offers the insured complete preventive medical care.

Preferred Provider Organization (PPO)

Under a Preferred Provider Organization plan, the insured is given a financial incentive to seek medical care from one of the medical providers in the insurer's selected network. For example, an insured typically pays a small co-payment for medical treatment by a network medical provider, e.g. 5 or 10 dollars.

If an insured elects to obtain medical care from a non-network medical provider, the procedure is similar to traditional health insurance in that the insured generally must pay the entire bill up-front and then submit the bill to the insurance carrier for reimbursement of a percentage of the medical bill, e.g., 80%. In addition, the insured may be charged a deductible for non-network medical expenses.

One advantage of a PPO is that the insured is permitted to seek medical care from a specialist without first obtaining permission from a primary physician. The specialist must be a network medical provider. However, preventive medical care may not be covered under a particular PPO plan.

Exclusive Provider Organization (EPO)

Exclusive Provider Organizations are a subset of the PPO with many of the features of the HMO. Under an EPO plan, it is even more costly to obtain medical treatment from a non-network medical provider because the insured is generally responsible for the entire cost without reimbursement.

Point of Service Plan (POS)

A Point of Service plan is similar to a PPO, however, the insured is required to obtain permission from a network primary care physician before seeking treatment from a specialist, even if the specialist is a network provider.

Nevertheless, under a POS plan, the insured still has the right to seek medical care from a non-network medical provider and be entitled to some reimbursement for the cost, although a deductible may apply. If, however, the primary care physician refers the insured to a non-network medical provider, the plan generally pays the costs.

A managed care health plan comparison chart is set forth at Appendix 6.

The Consolidated Omnibus Budget Reconciliation Act (COBRA)

Pursuant to the Consolidated Omnibus Budget Reconciliation Act of 1986 (COBRA), employers with 20 or more employees must offer the option of continuation of insurance coverage by the company's group health insurance plan, at the workers' own expense. Under the Act, an employee who is terminated for any reason other than "gross misconduct" is guaranteed the right to continue individual or family health care coverage under the former employer's group plan for as long as 18 months.

The same rule applies if the employee leaves their job voluntarily. In addition, an employee's spouse and dependent children are eligible for CO-

BRA coverage in the event of a divorce or the covered employee's death. However, despite the availability of COBRA health coverage, the costs of obtaining such coverage is quite high because the employee is responsible for paying the entire premium, including administrative costs.

Persons who elect COBRA coverage are generally those who have preexisting conditions, and who are concerned that their health care expenses without coverage will exceed the cost of the premiums. Because the premiums are usually so high, particularly for family coverage, many people take the chance that their health care expenses will be much lower than the cost of COBRA premiums.

Eligibility coverage under the Act also extends to employees in state and local government. Exemptions under the law exist for the District of Columbia, federal employees, and firms employing less than 20 people. In addition, employers with self-funded health plans are exempt from state regulation of their health plans.

Under the Act, employers have to notify employees of their right to COBRA coverage within a certain time period following termination. Employees who wish to elect COBRA coverage must do so within a specified time period.

The health insurance coverage offered under COBRA must be identical to the coverage enjoyed as an employee, although the employee has the right to drop "non-core" benefits such as dental or vision coverage.

Although coverage generally ends after 18 months, certain conditions may qualify the insured for an extension of coverage—e.g., the disability of the former employee—although the premiums may be increased for the additional time period.

The Family Medical Leave Act

Under The Family and Medical Leave Act (FMLA), an employer is required to maintain coverage under the company's group health plan for any employee who takes FMLA leave. The employee is entitled to the identical coverage he or she would have been provided if the employee had continued working and not taken FMLA leave. The coverage provided under the FMLA is not COBRA coverage. However, a COBRA qualifying event may occur when an employer's obligation to maintain health benefits under FMLA ceases, e.g., if the employee notifies the employer that he or she does not intend to return to work.

Medicare/Medicaid

Medicare and Medicaid are the two primary government- operated health insurance programs available to qualified individuals. Although changes to both programs are pending, following is a general outline of the eligibility requirements, and the coverage available under the programs.

Medicare

When a person reaches age 65, he or she usually becomes eligible for Medicare, the federal health insurance program administered by the United States Social Security Administration. Medicare is an entitlement program funded by payroll taxes.

Unfortunately, Medicare does not cover all health-related expenses, and it is wise to supplement Medicare with additional health insurance coverage. For example, Medicare does not pay for dentures and routine dental care, eyeglasses, hearing aids, prescription drugs, routine physical checkups, orthopedic devices, and non-skilled nursing home care—items that account for a considerable portion of medical expenses, particularly for senior citizens.

As set forth below, there are two parts to the Medicare policy: (i) Part A Hospitalization Coverage; and (ii) Part B Medical Coverage.

Part A Hospitalization Coverage

Part A of the medicare policy covers hospitalization, for which there is a designated deductible—i.e., an initial amount one must pay for their hospitalization before Medicare begins to pay any additional expenses. This amount—known as the hospital deductible—increases every January 1st. As of January 1, 1998, the hospital deductible amount was $764.

Part A is free to most people 65 and older. Persons who have been receiving Social Security disability benefits for a period of 24 months also qualify for Part A hospital coverage. Eligible persons receive a health insurance card, known as a Medicare card, to claim their benefits. Persons already receiving Social Security automatically receive Medicare cards as part of their Social Security benefits.

Part A hospital coverage helps pay for three basic kinds of care: (i) inpatient hospital care; (ii) inpatient care in a skilled nursing facility; and (iii) home health care. However, the duration of care per benefit period is limited. A benefit period begins when the patient first enters a hospital or other facility, and ends after he or she has been discharged from the facility for a continuous period of 60 days from the date of discharge. This rule is simply a measurement device. There is no limit to the number of periods in which one may receive benefits.

Part B Medical Coverage

Part B of the medicare policy covers health-related expenses, other than hospitalization, including certain physician services, outpatient hospital care, laboratory and diagnostic tests, and many other specified medical expenses not covered by Part A. Anyone who is eligible for Part A hospital coverage is eligible for Part B medical coverage, however, Part B is not free. There is a monthly premium that increases every January 1st. As of January 1, 1998, that amount was $43.80.

Part B medical coverage, unlike Part A, is based on a calendar year, rather than on benefit periods. The Part B medical coverage yearly deductible is $100.00 dollars. After the deductible is paid, Medicare pays 80% percent of the reasonable charges for covered services for the balance of the year.

The Qualified Medicare Beneficiary Program

Persons who receive Medicare and have income and resources below a certain amount may be eligible for the Qualified Medicare Beneficiary (QMB) program. Under the QMB program, the State pays Medicare premiums, deductibles and coinsurance for persons who qualify for the program.

Medigap Insurance

Medicare does not pay for all of an individual's medical expenses. Therefore, eligible Medicare recipients may also purchase supplemental coverage known as Medigap insurance. Medigap policies generally pay for medical-related expenses not reimbursed by Medicare, such as hospital deductibles and copayments.

Medigap policies are designed to supplement Medicare and generally do not cover long-term care, although some policies do provide for skilled nursing home care and at-home recovery care. Further information concerning Medigap insurance policies may be obtained from the National Insurance Consumer Helpline at (800) 942-4242.

Medicaid

Medicaid is a program designed to provide health services, including nursing home care, to persons who are financially eligible. Medicaid eligibility is determined by a number of factors, the most important of which is income level. To be eligible for Medicaid, one must first exhaust all of their assets and savings—not including their home—a process known as "spending down."

Only certain classes of individuals are eligible for Medicaid, including: (i) pregnant women; (ii) children from low- income households; (iii) elderly persons including those who, although eligible for Medicare, cannot afford it; and (iv) disabled persons.

Each state formulates and administers its own Medicaid program, following federal government guidelines, through matching federal funds based on the state's per capita income. Within these guidelines, states have considerable freedom in managing their own Medicaid program, thus coverage varies from state-to-state. For example, individual states set the financial eligibility criteria for Medicaid in their jurisdiction, which are often well below federally established poverty levels.

Medicaid offers more comprehensive coverage than Medicare. However, the program's low reimbursement levels discourages private medical providers from participating in the program.

Medicaid pays for costs not covered by Medicare for elderly persons who qualify for Medicare but cannot afford the Part A hospital deductible or Part B premium. Nevertheless, Medicaid is generally not an alternative resource to most persons in need of long-term care because of the stringent restrictions.

An exception exists under the spouse impoverishment provisions of Medicare, which provide that the spouse of a person receiving long-term care in a nursing home is permitted to keep a certain dollar amount of assets and income, and still be eligible for Medicaid. However, the amount one is allowed to retain is still very modest.

Long-Term Health Care Insurance

This section discusses the availability of an insurance policy to protect individuals in need of care over an extended period of time. Unlike acute care—short-term, recuperative care provided by a hospital—long-term care is the type of care given to persons who have become disabled or who suffer from a chronic illness.

Long-term care is often a concern for senior citizens. Although many senior citizens are able to live out their lives independently and in good health, many others have health care problems which render them infirm and dependent on others to help them with their daily activities.

In 1991, 7 million senior citizens were in need of long-term care. This number is expected to increase to almost 9 million by the year 2000. The majority of the cost of this care is borne by the patients and their families. This is particularly burdensome in the retirement years when most older persons are on fixed incomes.

Responding to this need, a large number of insurance companies have stepped in to fill the gap, providing a variety of insurance policies covering long-term care. If one is considering purchasing such a policy, it would be prudent to review the benefits being offered by the various companies in order to choose the policy that best fits your needs.

The Costs of Long-Term Care

With the exception of the Medicaid program, which has limited eligibility, much of what is covered under long-term health care insurance is either not covered at all, or only partially covered under Medicare or private health insurance policies. The cost of fully providing such care would be prohibitive. The average cost of care in a nursing home is estimated at $25,000 per year and more, depending on the facility, the location, and the level of care provided. Home care costs can range from $50 to $200 per day, again depending on the level of care and the number of hours provided.

Although long-term care insurance can be very helpful if it is ever needed, it can also be quite costly, ranging anywhere from $250 to over $2000 per year for the average senior citizen who is in good health. Before taking on this considerable expense, it would be wise to carefully assess one's individual situation and investigate all resources available from other programs. Some of the factors one should consider when assessing the need for long-term care insurance, include:

1. The individual's present financial situation and projected financial situation following retirement.

2. The individual's ability to afford long-term care insurance.

3. The programs the individual expects to be eligible for upon retirement and whether they will be able to meet his or her needs.

4. The likelihood that the individual will require long- term care in the future, based on his or her present health and family history.

5. The alternative resources the individual expects to have if long-term care is needed, such as family and friends, and the availability of community-based services.

Choosing a Long-Term Care Insurance Policy

Since long-term care insurance is a fairly recent development, one must be very careful in selecting and evaluating the various policies available, and inquiring into the background and stability of the companies offering such insurance.

Every policy generally contains some restrictions and limitations, and some policies may not be available to due to such factors as age and health. Carefully read all of the provisions of the policy before making your decision. If any of the provisions are unclear to you, one should seek professional assistance in understanding the policy. In general, the policy should be flexible enough to cover all levels of nursing home and home health care without undue restrictions, such as stipulations as to the facilities at which the individual can receive care. In addition, the policy should have a renewal guarantee.

Typical Long-Term Care Insurance Provisions

Although the provisions, limitations and restrictions of long-term care insurance policies may vary, there are a number of typical provisions found in most policies. Some of these provisions are discussed below.

Coverage

Long-term care insurance policies typically cover nursing home care. Some policies cover all levels of nursing home care—skilled nursing care, intermediate care, and custodial care—while others may cover only a certain level of care, such as skilled nursing care. It is best to purchase a policy that covers all levels of nursing home care, since long-term skilled nursing care is not usually needed. It is more likely that a person will need a lesser level of nursing home care, such as custodial care, over an extended period of time. Also be aware of any limitations or prerequisites to such care.

Home health care is generally provided for in long-term care insurance policies. Again, however, one must be aware of any limitations on the availability of such care. For example, some policies may only provide home health care after hospitalization, which may not be necessary in every case even though the individual may be in need of home health care services. In addition, long-term care insurance may include coverage for such services as assistance with household chores, shopping, transportation and personal hygiene, as well as long-term skilled nursing care.

Benefits

Most policies pay only a preset daily benefit for nursing home care or home health care, and the difference between the amount covered by the insurance and the actual costs of care is borne by the insured. Some policies allow the insured to pay higher premiums in return for higher daily benefits. When considering inflation, one must be aware that in many cases the benefits payable under the policy will not be increased. Therefore, the individual will be responsible for any escalation in the costs of care due to inflation.

To avoid this problem, one must shop around for a policy that provides for benefit increases over time due to inflation. One must also be aware of any limits the policy places on the duration of care and the benefits payable under the policy. Generally, policies that provide for a longer duration of care and benefits will be more costly.

Policy Restrictions

Most long-term care policies contain various restrictions. For example, a restriction on preexisting conditions—conditions that existed prior to the policy's effective date—typically denies the insured any benefits connected with those specific health conditions for a designated waiting period after the effective date of the policy.

Another restriction that often appears in long-term care insurance policies is the waiting period, known as the elimination period, during which the policy does not pay benefits. For example, if a policy specifies that benefits for home health care will begin on the 21st day, that means the insured is responsible for payment out-of-pocket for the first 20 days of home health care. Lower cost policies may contain waiting periods that are considerably longer. In considering a policy's waiting periods, you must determine whether it is worth the higher premium to insure that you will receive benefits at the earliest possible date.

To obtain further information on all aspects of long-term care, one should contact their State Office of Long-Term Care Ombudsman. A directory of the State Offices of Long-Term Care Ombudsman is set forth at Appendix 7.

CHAPTER 4:

AUTOMOBILE INSURANCE

In General

All states require an individual who registers a car to purchase automobile insurance. Automobile insurance generally protects the insured, the insured's property, and damages sustained to the person and property of individuals as a result of an accident involving the insured. Automobile insurance protects the insured from catastrophic financial losses if they are found to be at fault for an accident.

The Automobile Insurance Policy

Under an automobile insurance policy, the insured is generally known as the "first party," the insurance carrier is the "second party," and any injured persons are known as "third parties." Elements of coverage common to many automobile insurance policies include: (i) liability coverage; (ii) medical coverage; (iii) collision coverage; (iv) comprehensive coverage; and (v) uninsured motorists coverage, which are discussed further below.

Liability Coverage

Liability coverage indemnifies the insured for the cost of bodily injury and property damage losses sustained by a third party where the insured is determined to be at fault for the accident. The insurance carrier also bears the cost of the insured's legal defense.

Each state sets its own minimum liability insurance requirements. However, although purchasing the minimum would satisfy the legal requirements of the state, individuals with considerable assets should be aware that the state minimums are rarely adequate to cover significant losses, and may expose the insured to additional risk beyond the coverage provided by the policy.

Policy coverage limits are set forth as a series of three numbers, e.g., 50/100/50. The first number refers to the maximum bodily injury coverage per person (e.g., $50,000); the second number refers to the maximum total bodily injury coverage per accident (e.g., $100,000); and the third number refers to the upper limit of the insured's property damage protection (e.g., $50,000).

Thus, using the above policy limits, if an accident occurred involving the insured and a third party, where the insured was at fault, the insurance carrier would be liable for up to $50,000 in compensation to each third party for their bodily injuries. One injured person cannot receive more than $50,000 from the insurance carrier regardless of his or her injuries.

Further, if there were five injured persons, the total compensation for all five bodily injury claims cannot exceed a $100,000 payment by the insurance carrier. Thus, the insured would be responsible for the difference between the amounts paid by the insurance carrier, and the damages awarded the injured parties.

In addition, the insurance carrier's property damage exposure is limited to $50,000. Therefore, if the third party's automobile is totalled, and it happens to be worth $75,000, the insured would still be responsible for the difference.

A chart of the minimum automobile insurance liability limits by state is set forth at Appendix 8.

Medical Coverage

Medical coverage indemnifies the insured for medical expenses incurred by individuals covered under the policy—e.g., the insured and the insured's family. These expenses are known as "first party" expenses. Such expenses may arise as a result of accidents in the insured's vehicle, as well as accident's occurring in other vehicles driven with the owner's permission, and injuries sustained as pedestrians.

Medical expenses are covered regardless of liability, however, the insurance carrier retains the right to recoup such monies from any other party if it is determined that they are at fault for the accident.

Collision Coverage

Collision coverage pays the insured for the cost of damages sustained to the insured's vehicle above the policy deductible. In case of total loss, insurance companies will usually only pay, at a maximum, the "blue book" market value of the vehicle. Collision coverage is usually the most expensive type of insurance coverage, and is not mandatory. Generally, the higher the deductible, the lower the premium. If the insured's vehicle is damaged in an accident, and there is no other party at fault, the insured would have to pay the cost of repairs to the damaged vehicle. Although not mandated by law, collision coverage is generally required by the bank or finance company who leases or finances the vehicle, if applicable.

Comprehensive Coverage

Comprehensive coverage compensates the insured for damages sustained to the car that are not caused by an accident, e.g., fire, theft, vandalism or other natural disaster. Again, in case of total loss, insurance companies will pay, at a maximum, the "blue book" market value of the vehicle.

Although not mandated by law, comprehensive coverage is also generally required by the bank or finance company if the automobile is being leased or financed.

Uninsured Motorists Coverage

Uninsured motorists coverage compensates the insured for injuries sustained in accidents with individuals who have no automobile insurance.

Underinsured Motorists Coverage

Underinsured motorists coverage permits the insured to increase liability payments for personal injury and property damage they suffer where the other driver has insufficient coverage.

Supplemental Coverage

Some insurance carriers offer other types of supplemental automobile insurance coverage, including (i) roadside service coverage, e.g., towing and labor expenses; (ii) reimbursement for rental car expenses if the insured's vehicle is stolen or being repaired; and (iii) automobile replacement coverage which guarantees that the vehicle will be repaired or replaced regardless of the blue book value of the car.

The Cost of Automobile Insurance

Insurance rates may vary significantly based upon a number of factors, including but not limited to: (i) the type of car; (ii) the driver's record and experience; (iii) the driver's age and sex; (iv) the driver's place of residence—e.g., areas with high auto theft frequency will generally charge more for comprehensive coverage; and (v) the use of the car, e.g., insurance carriers generally charge a higher rate to individuals who drive their car to and from work.

State insurance departments periodically conduct and publish surveys concerning automobile insurance rates among different insurance companies, and the factors upon which the premiums are based. The reader is advised to check this information as a starting point when shopping around for the best insurance rates.

A directory of state insurance departments is set forth at Appendix 9.

Because the cost of automobile insurance may vary greatly among different insurance carriers, it is a good idea to comparison shop when purchasing automobile insurance. In addition to shopping around for the best rates, it is important to do some research into the reputation and track record of prospective insurance carriers. Some factors to consider would be the coverage available, and the manner and efficiency in which claims are handled. Information about consumer complaints may be obtained by contacting the state's consumer affairs department and the Better Business Bureau.

A directory of the major casualty and property insurance carriers is set forth at Appendix 10.

Available Discounts

Insurance carriers offer discounts to consumers under certain circumstances, including but not limited to:

1. Drivers with good records, e.g. no accidents or moving violations within a certain period of time.
2. Older drivers, e.g. 55+;
3. Car-pool drivers;
4. Multi-car discounts, e.g., households who insure more than one vehicle with the same insurance carrier;
5. Home/Car Discounts, e.g., insureds who insure both their home and car with the same insurance carrier;
6. Garaged car discounts;
7. Anti-theft device discounts; e.g. Car alarms;
8. Safety device discounts, e.g. air bags; and
9. Safety course completion discounts.

The availability and amount of the particular discount varies, therefore the reader is advised to check with their insurance carrier.

A chart representing the average automobile insurance premium by state is set forth at Appendix 11.

Shared Market Insurance Programs

Some individuals, due to their age, lack of experience, neighborhood, or negative driving record, have difficulty obtaining automobile insurance. Nevertheless, every state has some provision which guarantees such individuals automobile insurance even if an insurance carrier does not wish to provide coverage.

Coverage for drivers who present a considerable risk are usually handled in a pool to which all insurance carriers belong—known as a "shared" market. The insurance premiums may be very high and the coverage not as favorable as policies sold in the "voluntary" market. Approximately 20 percent of all drivers are insured in the "shared market"—also referred to as "assigned risk" programs in some states.

Processing the Auto Accident Claim

In order to facilitate the processing of the insured's claim through the insurance claims process, following are some guidelines one should consider when involved in an automobile accident.

1. Insist that the police be called to the scene of the accident so that an accurate report of the circumstances surrounding the accident can be recorded. Make sure the police officer takes down your version of the accident.

2. Exchange identification and insurance information with the other driver.

3. Report the accident to your insurance carrier. Your rates will generally not be affected if the accident was not your fault.

4. Review your policy carefully to make sure you understand its provisions and any instructions you must follow in case of an accident. The cover sheet of the policy—also known as the "declarations page"—sets forth the type of coverage and the policy limits. Also review the exclusions section of the policy which sets forth those items your insurance carrier does not cover. If you have any questions, contact your insurance carrier or broker.

If the accident involves property damage, it is important to obtain an estimate from an auto body repair shop. Unfortunately, cars are often declared "totalled"—i.e., a total loss—even though the monetary threshold used in determining the loss—usually market value—is far below the replacement cost of the automobile.

No-Fault Automobile Insurance

In General

No-fault automobile insurance, also known as personal injury protection (PIP), refers to an expanded type of medical coverage required by a number of states ("no-fault" states), and offered by many insurance carriers in states where no-fault is not mandated.

In addition to medical expenses, no-fault coverage typically includes compensation for lost wages; out-of-pocket expenses, such as the cost of drugs and travel expenses to and from necessary medical treatment; and payment for obtaining services that the injured person can no longer perform on their own, e.g. household help.

Prior to the introduction of no-fault insurance, traditional tort-based liability was the norm. The tort system requires the accident victim to prove that another party was responsible for causing the accident in order to recover damages. States began to enact no-fault laws as an attempt to reform the manner by which automobile accident victims were compensated.

Under this approach, emphasis is placed on compensating the injured without concern for assessing blame. It was hoped that no-fault laws would reduce the number of lawsuits and help to lower the cost of automobile insurance. However, the system proved to have its own shortcomings.

A Pure No-Fault System

Blame for the rise in insurance costs may be attributed to the fact that, although almost half of all jurisdictions passed some form of no-fault automobile legislation, not one jurisdiction enacted a pure no-fault system. Under a pure no- fault system, accident victims would receive substantial benefits to compensate them for their losses. However, they would have no legal right to pursue a lawsuit against the party responsible for the accident.

The only exceptions in a pure no-fault system would be very narrowly defined, such as those based on public policy grounds—e.g., if the responsible party intended to cause injury, or was driving under the influence of alcohol or drugs.

Opponents of a pure no-fault system argue that it violates the basic tort principle which holds the wrongdoer liable for his or her acts. They reason that no-fault legislation encourages careless driving by eliminating the deterrent effect of a potential lawsuit, and unfairly requires responsible drivers to purchase additional insurance to protect themselves from careless drivers.

Presently, there are no jurisdictions in the United States which have a pure no-fault system. Those which did enact some form of no-fault legislation found that the combined recoveries from the no-fault system and the available tort remedies actually increased automobile insurance premiums.

Thus, the expected savings due to a reduction in tort recoveries, which was expected to help finance the no-fault system, did not come to fruition.

Ironically, the outcome has, in many cases, increased compensation to accident victims beyond what they would have received under the tort-based system. Benefits are often duplicated and, as a result, insurance premiums have skyrocketed.

As a result of these drawbacks, and the unanticipated rise in insurance costs, some jurisdictions which had previously enacted no-fault legislation repealed their no-fault laws. This was due in large part to studies indicating that repeal of the no- fault law would lower the average insurance premium, which, according to recent statistics, appears to be the case in those jurisdictions.

Jurisdictions which either retained their tort-based systems, or which repealed their no-fault laws include: Alabama, Alaska, Arizona, California, Connecticut, Georgia, Idaho, Illinois, Indiana, Iowa, Louisiana, Maine, Mississippi, Missouri, Montana, Nebraska, Nevada, New Mexico, North Carolina, Ohio, Oklahoma, Rhode Island, South Carolina, Tennessee, Vermont, West Virginia and Wyoming.

Traditional Tort Liability

Prior to the enactment of no-fault insurance legislation, recovery for personal injuries sustained as a result of an automobile accident was subject to common law negligence rules—the "tort liability" system. This is still the law today in many jurisdictions.

Under this tort-based system, an accident victim recovers damages for both economic and non-economic damages from the party who was responsible for causing the accident (the "third party"), and recovers under the bodily injury protection coverage of that party's insurance policy. Such damages include property damage, medical expenses, lost wages and general damages, e.g. pain and suffering.

Problems with the tort-based system prompted a need for insurance reform. For example, as in any personal injury case, the accident victim must prove the responsible party's negligence in order to prevail—a time consuming process. Contributory and comparative negligence rules also apply which, depending on the jurisdiction, may limit or prevent the plaintiff's recovery. Further, the liability limits of the wrongdoer's liability insurance, if in fact there is insurance, may be so low that it does not fully compensate the accident victim for his or her losses. In all jurisdictions, except Michigan, property damage claims are still subject to the traditional tort system.

The No-Fault/Tort Liability System

As previously discussed, no jurisdiction has yet enacted pure no-fault legislation. Most jurisdictions which have adopted a no-fault system have also developed a statutory basis for accident victims to maintain a tort action against the responsible party if certain criteria are met. Under such a combined system, the accident victim receives some no-fault economic loss benefits from his or her own insurance carrier regardless of fault.

Presently, there are twenty-four jurisdictions which have some sort of automobile no-fault law. They include: Arkansas, Colorado, Delaware, District of Columbia, Florida, Hawaii, Kansas, Kentucky, Maryland, Massachusetts, Michigan, Minnesota, New Hampshire, New Jersey, New York, North Dakota, Oregon, Pennsylvania, South Dakota, Texas, Utah, Virginia, Washington and Wisconsin.

No-fault insurance requires individuals to purchase their own "first party" personal injury protection ("PIP"). If they are injured in an accident, they are able to recover their economic losses directly from their own insurance carrier, regardless of who actually caused the accident. Economic loss refers to medical expenses, lost earnings and expenses for substitute services, such as household help, etc. Thus, accident victims do not have to rely on successfully suing the party responsible for the accident in order to receive needed compensation.

Economic damages are readily provable—e.g., by medical bills and employment records, and are thus easy to calculate. However, if the accident victim is reimbursed by a collateral source, such as disability compensation, duplicate benefits would not be permitted for the same expense. Net economic loss represents the accident victim's actual out-of-pocket expenses resulting from the injury.

Under no-fault, first party benefits do not reimburse the accident victim for non-economic damages, such as pain and suffering. However, under the combined system, the accident victims may, under certain defined circumstances, recover non-economic damages in a tort action if they are able to prove that another party caused the accident. Non-economic damages are not as easy to prove and are left to a jury to determine.

A problem which stems from this overlap of systems is the tendency to encourage accident victims to inflate their claims of medical expenses and lost wages so that they meet the threshold which permits them to sue in tort. Because tort recoveries for pain and suffering are often a multiple of the victim's economic loss, he or she may seek additional medical treatment and leave from work. Thus, both the no-fault benefits and tort recoveries for the individual are increased. There is really no incentive for the accident victim to settle for no-fault benefits alone.

In fact, the accident victims in a combined system are able to more comfortably pursue a tort claim because they are receiving first party benefits from their own insurer, whereas accident victims in traditional tort liability jurisdictions have more of an incentive to settle their claims because they are not receiving any interim financial benefits.

Under no-fault, the accident victim may be required to give his or her insurance carrier the right of subrogation—i.e., the right to sue the responsible party.

A sample subrogation agreement in a no-fault claim is set forth at Appendix 12.

Coverage

All no-fault statutes must particularly identify the coverage which is included in its system. This would typically include the type of vehicles covered and their uses, and the persons covered by the insurance.

Covered Vehicles

In general, all private passenger vehicles registered and insured in the particular jurisdiction would be covered under the jurisdiction's no-fault statutes. Generally, motorcycles and mopeds, farm and construction equipment, and government vehicles are excluded from coverage.

An excluded vehicle is usually not required to maintain no-fault insurance. However, this subjects the vehicle's owner to tort actions, and generally prevents injured occupants of the vehicle from receiving any first party benefits.

Covered Uses

Covered usage is generally defined as the use, operation or maintenance of the vehicle. In order to recover no-fault benefits, it must be determined that the injuries sustained by the accident victim arose out of such use, operation or maintenance of the vehicle. Exclusions from covered uses may be set forth in the jurisdiction's no-fault statute, or in the insurance contract, and generally include conduct such as: (i) driving while under the influence of alcohol or drugs; (ii) driving a stolen vehicle; (iii) fleeing from arrest or committing a felony; (iv) racing, or (v) any use intended to cause injury to oneself or another.

Covered Persons

Most no-fault systems cover: (i) the named insured; (ii) family members of the insured's household; (iii) occupants of the insured vehicle; and (iv) pedestrians who may be injured by the insured vehicle. Employees of a corporation may also be entitled to first party benefits unless specifically excluded from the corporate insurance policy.

No-Fault Insurance Claim Procedure

Most no-fault systems reimburse accident victims for their basic economic loss, with varying limitations. In order to claim no-fault benefits under the insured's policy—known as "first party benefits"—the insured must file a no-fault claim application with the insurance carrier within a certain number of days following the accident.

In some cases, all or part of a claim is denied or not timely paid. If that occurs, the insured may be able to seek intervention from the state insurance department or resolve the dispute voluntarily through arbitration. If these methods fail, the insured may have to engage a lawyer to sue the insurance carrier and recover the no-fault benefits.

A sample complaint to recover no-fault insurance benefits is set forth at Appendix 13.

As discussed below, no-fault benefits compensate the victim for such items as medical expenses, lost wages, the cost of engaging substitute services, survivor or death benefits, and funeral and burial expenses.

Medical Benefits

Medical benefits generally cover the hospital, doctor and nursing bills. Also covered would be necessary rehabilitation, such as physical therapy. Medical expenses must be "reasonable"—e.g., comply with a statutory fee schedule—and generally must be incurred within a certain prescribed time period following the accident. The insurance carrier may also require the accident victim to undergo independent medical examinations—i.e., medical examinations by physicians who are selected by the insurer. A claimant who refuses to submit to these examinations is subject to loss of benefits.

Lost Earnings

No-fault insurance does not provide an accident victim with unlimited reimbursement for lost wages, but does compensate the victim for most or all of their lost wages according to the jurisdiction's statutory scheme. The wages must be verified by the victim's employer, or if self-employed, by income tax records. The no-fault carrier may require the claimant to pursue disability benefits from available collateral sources—e.g., workers compensation insurance—so as not to duplicate compensation.

Survivor Benefits

In the case of a deceased accident victim, benefits may be available to survivors—usually designated as the spouse and children of the victim—in the form of lost wages of the victim, and payment for substitute services for those that would have been performed by the accident victim. Some jurisdictions pay a flat first-party death benefit to the survivors, who are also permitted to seek further recovery in a wrongful death action against the negligent party.

The Add-On Jurisdictions

Some jurisdictions, in an effort to prevent duplication of benefits, have enacted what is known as "add-on" legislation. In the "add-on" jurisdictions, accident victims are permitted to both (i) receive no-fault benefits; and (ii) pursue a tort action. However, the no-fault benefits cannot be duplicated by the tort recovery, thus, the damages awarded in a tort action would be reduced accordingly.

Presently, the following jurisdictions have enacted "add-on" legislation: Arkansas, Delaware, District of Columbia, Maryland, New Hampshire, Oregon, South Dakota, Texas, Virginia, West Virginia and Wisconsin.

Freedom of Choice

Freedom of choice refers to the more recent trend toward allowing the customer to decide which type of insurance—no-fault or tort liability—they would like to purchase (the "choice" system). There are variations on the basic options which further define the purchaser's choice, such as the extent to which a tort remedy would be available, e.g. in all instances, or only for certain defined categories of serious injury.

Generally, purchasers who choose to give up their right to maintain tort actions are rewarded with lower premiums, and purchasers who want to retain full rights to bring tort actions pay higher premiums. Presently, three jurisdictions offer some type of choice system: Kentucky, New Jersey and Pennsylvania.

In addition, as set forth below, federal legislation—The Auto Reform Choice Act of 1997—is presently pending which would provide a choice-based system nationwide.

The Auto Choice Reform Act of 1997

Federal legislation is presently pending in both the Senate and the House of Representatives which would change automobile insurance coverage nationwide. Based on its findings, Congress has blamed the tort liability insurance system for, among other things: (i) excessive insurance rates; (ii) failure to provide compensation commensurate with loss; (iii) unreasonable delay in payment of losses; (iv) excessive legal fees; (v) fraud in the claims process; and (vi) fraud and abuse of health care resources.

To remedy these problems, Congress is attempting to pass the Auto Choice Reform Act of 1997, which would permit purchasers of automobile insurance to choose between two insurance systems: (i) The Personal Protection System; and (ii) The Tort Maintenance System.

According to sponsors of the bill, the Act offers consumers the choice of opting out of the pain and suffering litigation pool, and consumers who elect to opt out will be rewarded with substantial savings on automobile insurance premiums. The Act does not propose to abolish the right to sue nor eliminate the concept of fault within the legal system. However, it does allow drivers to decide how they want to be insured.

The Tort Maintenance System

A driver who wants to be covered for pain and suffering would essentially buy the same type of insurance that they currently carry—and would recover, or fail to recover, in the same way that they do today. The only change for tort drivers would be that, in the event that they are hit by a personal protection driver, the tort driver would recover both economic and noneconomic damages from his or her own insurance policy. This supplemental first-party policy for tort drivers will be called tort maintenance coverage.

The Personal Injury Protection System

If a driver wants to opt-out of pain and suffering coverage, he or she chooses the personal protection system. Drivers choosing this system would be guaranteed prompt recovery of their economic losses, up to the levels of their own insurance policy. These drivers would give up recovery of pain and suffering damages in exchange for immunity from pain and suffering lawsuits. Personal protection drivers would achieve substantially reduced premiums because the personal protection system would dramatically reduce pain and suffering damages; fraud; and most attorney fees.

Nevertheless, under both insurance systems, the injured party whose economic losses exceed his own coverage will have the right to sue the responsible party for the excess. Moreover, tort drivers will retain the right to sue each other for both economic and noneconomic loss.

The full text of the Auto Choice Reform Act of 1997 is set forth at Appendix 14.

CHAPTER 5:

HOMEOWNER INSURANCE

In General

Homeowner insurance refers to a contract between an insurance company and a homeowner, under which the homeowner is protected from losses that result from certain conditions. These conditions are referred to as "perils," as defined in the policy.

Homeowner insurance policies are basically uniform throughout the United States in terms of the coverage they provide. Homeowner policies generally insure both the dwelling and personal property. Renter and condominium owner policies only insure the contents of the dwelling because the landlord or condominium association usually purchases a separate policy that insures the dwelling itself.

Many basic policies do not include protection for certain natural disasters, such as earthquakes or floods. As set forth below, homeowners who live in areas that are particularly susceptible to a certain type of natural disaster are advised to obtain a supplemental policy to cover such natural disasters.

If a homeowner sustains a covered loss, it is important to contact the insurance carrier or agent as soon as possible. Most major insurance companies have a central number for reporting a claim, which is then forwarded to the appropriate local office for processing and investigation.

Six Basic Types of Homeowner Insurance Policies

As set forth below, there are six basic types of insurance policies commonly offered to homeowners, which cover multiple perils.

The HO-1 Policy

The HO-1 homeowner policy is a basic policy which generally covers the dwelling and personal property from eleven (11) enumerated perils: fire or lightning; windstorm or hail; explosion; riot or civil commotion; aircraft; vehicles; smoke; vandalism or malicious mischief; theft; damage by glass or safety glazing material that is part of a building; and volcanic eruption.

The HO-2 Policy

The HO-2 homeowner policy generally covers the dwelling and personal property from seventeen (17) enumerated perils, which includes the eleven (11) perils covered under the HO-1 policy, plus six (6) additional perils: falling objects; weight of ice, snow or sleet; three categories of water-related damage from home utilities or appliances; and electrical surge damage.

The HO-3 Policy

The HO-3 homeowner policy offers the homeowner more extensive coverage. The HO-3 policy covers all of the seventeen (17) perils covered under the HO-2 policy, in addition to any peril not specified in the policy. Coverage exclusions exist for flood, earthquake, war and nuclear accident—perils which generally require the purchase of a supplemental insurance policy.

The HO-4 Policy

The HO-4 policy refers to Renter's Insurance. Renter's insurance covers personal property only from the seventeen (17) perils covered under the HO-2 homeowner policy. It is wise for renters to obtain this type of coverage because the insurance purchased by the landlord may only cover the dwelling.

The HO-6 Policy

The HO-6 policy covers condominium owners. The HO-6 policy also covers personal property only from the seventeen (17) perils covered under the HO-2 homeowner policy. Again, it is wise for condominium owners to obtain this type of coverage because the insurance purchased by the condominium association may only cover the dwelling.

The HO-8 Policy

The HO-8 policy refers to coverage available for older homes. Generally, these policies cover the dwelling and property from eleven (11) perils covered under the HO-1 homeowner policy. However, the HO-8 policy usually does not reimburse the homeowner for the replacement cost of the dwelling, but will generally only pay for repairs or actual cash value. The reasoning for this limitation on coverage is that certain older homes may have historic or architectural value which renders the replacement value significantly higher than the market value.

All six policy types listed above routinely include liability coverage, and exclude coverage for damages caused by earthquakes and floods. In some areas, windstorm damage may also be excluded.

Liability Coverage

Liability coverage protects the homeowner from lawsuits filed by others, e.g., a visitor who falls on the homeowner's property. Liability insurance pays the injured party for their losses, as well as the cost of the legal defense.

Homeowners who have considerable assets are advised to maintain a high level of liability coverage in their policy to protect their interests. In addition, policies known as "umbrella" policies offer excess liability coverage on both one's homeowner and automobile policies, and are relatively inexpensive considering the additional coverage they provide.

Supplemental Coverage

As set forth above, standard homeowner insurance policies do not insure against losses caused by floods and earthquakes, or against windstorms in areas which are prone to significant damage as a result of such storms. This is because the nature of insurance is to quantify risks, and where those risks are high, to set premiums that will still provide a reasonable return of profit to the insurance company after claims are paid.

Natural disasters—such as floods, earthquakes and windstorms—are unpredictable, which makes the insurance carrier's attempt to quantify the risks more difficult. However, certain trends will make specific regions more vulnerable to catastrophe than other areas, requiring the homeowner to purchase supplemental insurance coverage.

Flood Insurance

Flooding is the second most common natural disaster after fire damage. The standard homeowner policy does not cover flooding. The federal government, under the auspices of The Federal Emergency Management Agency (FEMA), oversees an extensive federally-funded insurance program—The National Flood Insurance Program—which is designed to address the problem of flooding, in conjunction with local communities and private insurance companies.

Local regions are entitled to participated in the National Flood Insurance Program provided the local government develops flood programs which meet the FEMA requirements. Flood policies are available through private insurance carriers. Further information and referrals can be obtained from the National Flood Insurance Program by calling 800-427-4661.

As of June 1997, all standard flood insurance policies began including an endorsement for Increased Cost of Compliance coverage (ICC). ICC is a mandatory part of a standard flood insurance policy, so if a homeowner wants flood insurance, he or she must pay for ICC coverage.

ICC coverage is designed to make sure that the flood damages will not reoccur. For example, ICC helps to cover the costs of rebuilding a structure in a manner which will prevent its destruction from floodwaters.

According to the National Flood Insurance Program, there are two cases in which a homeowner can file an ICC claim: (i) substantial damage; and (ii) repetitive damage. Substantial damage refers to repair costs that are approximately 50% or more of the structure's pre-damage market value. Repetitive damage exists if a flood has damaged the structure at least two times in the past 10 years, and the repair costs average approximately 25% of the structure's pre-damage market value.

If it is determined that a homeowner is eligible to file an ICC claim, there are generally four options available to comply with the floodplain management ordinance:

1. Elevation - Raising the structure to higher ground;
2. Relocation - Moving the structure to a safer area;
3. Demolition - Removing the flood-damaged structure; and
4. Floodproofing - Making the structure waterproof.

Earthquake Insurance

Earthquake coverage is provided by private insurers. Because the damage claims which usually accompany an earthquake can be financially staggering, earthquake insurance is very costly. Thus, even in susceptible areas, such as California, earthquake insurance is only purchased by a minority of homeowners.

Windstorms

In general, damage caused by windstorms are covered in the standard homeowner policy. However, in particularly susceptible areas, such as coastal areas where storms such as hurricanes can be devastating, an insurance carrier may require residents to purchase supplemental windstorm coverage.

Seven states along the Atlantic and Gulf coasts—Alabama, Florida, Louisiana, Mississippi, North Carolina, South Carolina, and Texas—operate beach and windstorm insurance plans. These plans ensure that homeowners in coastal areas can get insurance coverage against damage from hurricanes and other windstorms.

Replacement Value Coverage

It is preferable for the homeowner to insure the dwelling and its contents for the replacement value. The replacement value usually differs from a property's market value, or the depreciated cash value of any personal property. In addition, it is wise to purchase a policy which automatically provides for adjustments due to inflation.

A bank or financial institution which holds a mortgage on a property will require the homeowner to maintain insurance during the term of the loan. Many homeowners mistakenly assume that whatever the bank requires is sufficient. However, the coverage which may be acceptable to the lender does not necessarily afford adequate protection to the homeowner. The lender is generally only concerned that their exposure is protected.

Therefore, the homeowner is advised to carefully consult with their insurance agent concerning their insurance needs, and the type of policy which will provide them with the most coverage at an affordable price.

Personal Property Coverage

The basic homeowner policy generally insures personal property for approximately one-half of the value of the dwelling. However, standard policies may not even remotely provide enough compensation for the replacement cost of the average home electronics system or jewelry collection. In addition, if the homeowner operates a business out of the dwelling, equipment and related business assets may not be satisfactorily covered under a basic policy.

The homeowner is advised to purchase supplemental coverage—known as "floaters"—that will provide additional coverage for certain categories of personal property. The cost of obtaining this extra protection is relatively small considering the coverage it provides. A homeowner policy generally provides other types of coverage, including protection from thefts which occur when the insured is away from the home.

If a homeowner purchases a policy with a higher deductible—i.e., the out-of-pocket cost borne by the homeowner before the insurer is obligated to provide compensation—he or she may receive a substantial deduction on the annual premium.

CHAPTER 6:

WORKERS' COMPENSATION INSURANCE

In General

When an employee suffers a work-related injury or illness, and as a result becomes disabled and unable to work, he or she may be entitled to receive certain benefits under a system known as workers' compensation. As more fully set forth in this almanac, the Federal government and every state administers some type of workers' compensation program according to its own statutory scheme.

Because statutory provisions vary depending on the particular jurisdiction, the reader is advised to check the law of his or her own jurisdiction concerning specific questions. This almanac sets forth a general discussion of workers' compensation law applicable to most jurisdictions. Presently, the Federal Government, all 50 states, Puerto Rico, the U.S. Virgin Islands, American Samoa and Guam, have workers' compensation laws.

Purpose

As set forth by the U.S. Chamber of Commerce in its 1995 Analysis of Workers' Compensation Laws, the following six basic objectives underlie workers' compensation laws:

1. To provide sure, prompt and reasonable income and medical benefits to work-accident victims, or income benefits to their dependents, regardless of fault;

2. To provide a single remedy and reduce court delays, costs and workloads arising out of personal injury litigation;

3. To relieve public and private charities of financial drains incident to uncompensated industrial accidents;

4. To eliminate payment of fees to lawyers and witnesses as well as time-consuming trials and appeals;

5. To encourage maximum employer interest in safety and rehabilitation through appropriate experience-rating mechanisms; and

6. To promote frank study of causes of accidents—rather than concealment of fault—reducing preventable accidents and human suffering.

State versus Federal Coverage

Most workers are covered by their own state's workers' compensation program unless they fall under those categories entitled to Federal coverage. Federal statutes have been enacted to provide coverage for certain classes of employees. The Federal Employees Compensation Program protects U.S. Government civilian employees; The Longshore and Harborworkers' Compensation Act protects maritime workers and certain other classes of workers; and the Black Lung Act protects coal miners.

Employer Immunity

As stated above, an employer who maintains workers' compensation insurance coverage for his or her employees is generally immune from employee lawsuits for work-related injuries or illnesses. There are some exceptions to this general immunity. For example, an employer who intentionally causes injury to an employee is generally not immune from a lawsuit.

The workers' compensation system was established so that disabled employees would not risk financial ruin and the uncertainty of a lawsuit. Employers benefit by avoiding the time and expense of litigation by making sure their workers receive benefits for work-related disabilities. Depending on the jurisdiction, workers' compensation laws may be either compulsory or elective.

Compulsory Workers' Compensation Laws

The majority of states have enacted compulsory workers' compensation laws. This means that employers are required to maintain workers' compensation coverage for their employees. Employers who fail to maintain the required insurance may be sued by the employee, and are liable for damages. Depending on the jurisdiction, non-complying employers may be further penalized.

Elective Workers' Compensation Laws

A minority of jurisdictions, including New Jersey, South Carolina and Texas, have elective workers' compensation laws. Under an elective law, the employer may choose to reject the workers' compensation system. However, if a suit for damages is brought by an injured employee, the employer cannot assert the three common law defenses of contributory negligence, assumption of risk, or fellow servant negligence doctrines.

Insurance Coverage

In general, most states require employers to maintain workers' compensation insurance for their employees, unless there is a statutory exception. Such insurance may be: (i) purchased from a State Insurance Fund; (ii) purchased from an authorized private insurance carrier; or (iii) provided by an employer under a self-insurance program.

State Insurance Funds

In a minority of jurisdictions, employers are required to obtain insurance through a state insurance fund. Privately obtained workers' compensation insurance is not permitted, although some of these jurisdictions do permit employer self- insurance. Although state insurance funds are generally adequately funded, they are criticized for their inefficiency, such as the timeliness in making compensation payments.

Private Insurance Carriers

The majority of states permit employers to obtain private workers' compensation coverage. Employers are free to choose from any number of private insurance companies that offer this coverage.

Self-Insured Employers

Approximately 48 states permit self-insurance. A self- insured employer assumes liability for workers' compensation, and generally sets up a reserve fund to pay benefits to disabled employees. Self-insurance usually requires authorization by the appropriate State Workers' Compensation Board officials. The employer seeking to be self-insured must demonstrate that it has the financial ability to carry the associated risks.

A Directory of State Workers' Compensation Boards is set forth at Appendix 15.

CHAPTER 7:

UNEMPLOYMENT INSURANCE

In General

Due to a number of economic factors, the long-held concept of "job security" is rare today. Major companies are engaged in massive lay-offs, and many jobs have been exported overseas. Absent an employment contract, employers are generally permitted to discharge an employee, with or without cause, provided the discharge is not illegal under any statutes which prohibit discrimination.

In order to assist individuals who find themselves unemployed, the government operates a program designed to provide benefits to most workers out of work due to no fault of their own. The unemployment insurance program operates under federal and state law. The program was established by the federal Social Security Act of 1935. Much of the federal program is implemented through the Federal Unemployment Tax Act.

To support the unemployment compensation systems a combination of federal and state taxes are levied upon employers. The proceeds from the unemployment taxes are deposited in an Unemployment Trust Fund. Each state has a separate account in the Fund to which deposits are made. State unemployment insurance tax is determined and controlled by the employer based on its own unemployment experience.

The Federal Government provides funding for benefits for unemployed federal employees and ex-military personnel. The Railroad Unemployment Insurance Act provides unemployment compensation for workers in the railroad industry who lose their jobs.

Almost all wage and salary workers are now covered by the joint Federal-State system. State agencies administer the programs within minimum guidelines established by Federal statute. Eligibility, payment amounts and benefit periods are determined by each state. The state processes the applications and dispenses the payments.

As agents of the Federal Government, the states also pay benefits to ex-servicemembers with recent active service in the Armed Forces, benefits to former civilian federal employees, and workers who lose their jobs as a result of the nation's trade policies or who lose jobs due to a natural disaster.

Eligibility for Unemployment Compensation

General Eligibility Requirements

The following criteria must be met in order to be eligible to receive unemployment benefits in most states:

1. The claimant must meet the state requirements for wages earned or time worked during a one year period prior to the claim.

2. The claimant must have become unemployed through no fault of their own.

3. The claimant must be able to work, i.e., physically and mentally capable of working every day of the week for which he or she is claiming benefits.

4. The claimant must be available for work, i.e., ready to start a job immediately and available for work every day of the week for which he or she is claiming benefits.

5. The claimant must actively seek work, i.e., for each week of benefits claimed, he or she must make an active search for work and do all that is reasonable to secure reemployment.

Continuing Eligibility Requirements

In order to remain eligible for benefits, the claimant must follow these rules:

1. The claimant must report to the local unemployment insurance claims office or employment service office on the day and at the appointed time. Failure to report may result in a denial of benefits.

2. The claimant must not refuse any offer of suitable work or risk loss of benefits.

3. The claimant must continue to meet the general eligibility requirements set forth above.

Disqualification

If any of the following conditions apply, the claimant may be disqualified from receiving benefits, either indefinitely or for a set period of time:

1. The claimant voluntarily quits their job without good cause, or voluntarily chooses to retire;

2. The claimant was terminated from their job because of misconduct;

3. The claimant's unemployment is due to a labor dispute; or

4. The claimant refuses suitable work.

A claimant who is denied benefits is entitled to appeal this decision to the appropriate administrative agency.

Filing a Claim for Unemployment Insurance Benefits

In order to avoid financial hardship, a discharged or laid off employee should immediately apply for unemployment benefits with the agency that administers the state's unemployment insurance program. Swift action is necessary to offset some of the lost income because there is usually a delay of several weeks or more before the first unemployment check is received, and savings can quickly dissipate under such circumstances. In addition, no payments will be made for the time period prior to filing the claim, even though the claimant may have been unemployed during that time.

One must file their claim with a local office of the agency that administers the state's unemployment insurance program. It is important to bring information concerning former employment, such as addresses and dates of employment. Failure to supply complete and accurate information may delay processing of the claim.

Claimants are generally required to register for employment with the state's employment service office. The service will assist the claimant in finding work at no charge. The service also assists claimants by referring them to job training programs, conducting workshops, and assisting claimants in preparing a resume.

Payment of Benefits

Unemployment insurance pays benefits to qualified workers who are unemployed and looking for work, ensuring that at least a significant proportion of the necessities of life, such as food, clothing and housing, will be met while the individual searches for employment.

Benefits under state unemployment insurance programs are generally paid for 26 weeks in most states. In periods of very high unemployment in individual states, benefits are payable for as many as 13 to 20 additional weeks. These "extended benefits" are funded on a shared basis between Federal and state resources.

Unemployment benefits are generally paid for a seven- day period beginning on either a Sunday or Monday, and ending on either a Saturday or Sunday. The weekly benefit amount is generally about fifty percent of the amount the claimant earned while employed. Each state has a maximum benefit amount. Unemployment compensation benefits must be reported on the claimant's income tax return.

Disaster Unemployment Assistance

Section 410 of the Robert T. Stafford Disaster Relief and Emergency Assistance Amendments of 1988 created a program for the payment of unemployment assistance to individuals whose unemployment is the direct result of a major disaster, as declared by the President of the United States.

A claimant may be eligible for disaster unemployment assistance benefits if:

1. The claimant worked in, or was scheduled to begin work in, a county declared as a federal disaster county; and
2. The claimant cannot work as a direct result of the disaster; and
3. The work the claimant can't perform is their primary source of income and livelihood; and
4. The claimant doesn't qualify for regular unemployment insurance from any state. If so, the claimant must file under that program.

Disaster unemployment assistance benefits are normally one-half of the individual's average weekly wage—i.e., gross wages for workers and net wages for the self-employed claimants—during the previous tax year, up to a statutory maximum. Weekly disability unemployment assistance payments are reduced by gross income from grain, livestock, dairy or produce sales; wages from work or fees for services; social security benefits; and private income protection insurance.

Benefits are payable only during the time the claimant cannot work as a direct result of the major disaster. They are no longer eligible once they return to work or begin to perform services like those normally done during that time of the year. Disaster unemployment assistance benefits cannot be paid past the end of the disaster assistance period even if there is a balance remaining in the claim. A disaster assistance period normally lasts approximately 26 weeks.

Extended Benefits Program

The Unemployment Insurance Extended Benefits Program is a program the Federal government helps finance for states with high unemployment. Within the Unemployment Trust Fund there are accounts for extended unemployment compensation. During economic recessions the federal government has provided emergency assistance to allow states to extend the time for which individuals can receive benefits. This is accomplished by passing a temporary law which authorizes the transfer of money to a state from the extended unemployment account. The ability of a state to tap into this emergency system is usually dependent on the employment rate reaching a designated percentage within the state.

The Extended Benefits program provides an extra fifty percent of regular benefits—up to 13 extra weeks—while the high unemployment continues. Some states may offer eighty percent of benefits—i.e., 20 weeks—under some circumstances. The amount of compensation is the same amount as the compensation under regular benefits. If the program goes into effect all potentially eligible claimants are notified.

The Extended Benefits Program requires the claimant to conduct a more intensive work search, and has tighter rules on work refusal. In addition, not everyone who qualifies for regular benefits can receive extended benefits because the base period wage requirements are slightly different. Claimants may obtain a more detailed explanation of the special requirements from their local state unemployment agency.

Trade Adjustment Assistance Program

The Federal Trade Act provides special benefits under the Trade Adjustment Assistance program to those workers who are laid off or have their hours reduced because their employer is adversely affected by increased imports from other countries. Benefits known as "trade readjustment allowances" are paid to persons whose jobs are affected by foreign imports.

The North American Free Trade Agreement (NAFTA) provides special benefits under the NAFTA Transitional Adjustment Assistance (NAFTA-TAA) program to those who were laid off or had hours reduced because their employer was adversely affected by increased imports from Mexico or Canada or because their employer shifted production to either of these countries.

These benefits include paid training for a new job, financial help in making a job search in other areas, or relocation assistance to an area where jobs are more plentiful. Those who qualify may be entitled to special weekly benefits after their regular unemployment compensation is exhausted.

A petition for trade adjustment assistance must be filed with the U.S. Department of Labor (DOL). If the DOL approves and certifies the petition, the affected worker will be entitled to file a claim under the TAA or NAFTA-TAA program.

Unemployment Compensation for Federal Employees

Unemployment Compensation for Federal Employees is a benefit program for unemployed federal employees. Funding comes from the federal government and is distributed through state agencies. Federal wages are not reported to a state unemployment compensation agency until a claim is filed.

The claimant's federal wages will be "assigned" to the state of the last duty station or the state of residency if: (i) the duty station was outside the U.S; or (ii) the covered work was done in the state after leaving federal service; or (iii) the employer was the Federal Emergency Management Agency (FEMA).

Benefit amounts and duration are determined by the law of the state in which the claim is made. Federal wages assigned to another state may be transferred to the resident state under the Combined Wage Claim program.

When a claim is filed following a period of federal employment, the claimant must bring all forms the federal agency furnished upon departure. These include the SF-8 "Notice to Federal Employees About Unemployment Compensation" and the "Notification of Personnel Action." The claimant should also bring proof of the federal wages, if available.

Unemployment Compensation for Ex-Servicemembers

Unemployment Compensation for Ex-Servicemembers is a benefit program for ex-military personnel which provides weekly income to meet their basic needs while searching for employment. Those who were on active duty with a branch of the U.S. military may be entitled to unemployment benefits based on that service. The military wages are assigned to the state where they first file a new claim after separation from active duty. The claimant must meet the following requirements:

1. The claimant must have been separated under honorable conditions; and

2. The claimant must have completed a full term of service or, if released early, the release must have been for a qualifying reason; or

3. The claimant must have served on active duty in reserve status as a member of a National Guard or Reserve component continuously for 90 or more days.

Compensation benefits are paid under the same conditions as benefits based on other employment. However, military wages, for claims purposes, are determined by pay grade at the time of separation. A wage table furnished by the federal government which shows the equivalent civilian wage for each military pay grade is used to make this determination.

Information the military furnishes about length of service and the reason for separation is considered as final and binding. If any of this information is incorrect on the servicemember's DD-214 form, or other military documents, it is the responsibility of the claimant to contact the service to have the information reviewed and corrected.

Military benefits cannot be paid for any week for which the claimant received allowances from the Department of Veterans Affairs under Chapters 31 or 35 of Title 38 of the U.S. Code. These chapters provide subsistence allowances for vocational rehabilitation training and educational assistance allowances to war orphans and widows or, in some cases, children and spouses of permanent, totally disabled veterans. Benefits can also be reduced or denied because of pay for unused leave, pension, severance pay, or retirement pay.

CHAPTER 8:

SOCIAL SECURITY

In General

Social Security is a national program administered by the Social Security Administration, whereby employees and self- employed persons pay contributions, known as social security taxes, into the program during their working years. The amount of these taxes, which is determined by Congress, is a percentage of one's gross salary, up to a designated limit. This tax deduction is often designated as "FICA" on the employee's payroll stub. The employer is also required to pay social security taxes based on the employee's gross salary.

Social Security taxes are used to pay for all Social Security benefits, including a portion of the Medicare insurance coverage. The money Social Security takes in far exceeds the money it spends. The excess, called the "reserve," is pooled into special trust funds. The money in those trust funds is invested in Treasury bonds, which the government, by law, is required to pay back with interest.

Although Social Security is most often thought of as a retirement program, many persons are eligible to receive Social Security benefits before retirement age. When a person's earnings stop or are reduced because he or she retires, dies, or becomes disabled, monthly cash benefits are paid to replace part of the earnings the person or his or her dependent family has lost. Although a person may thus be eligible for Social Security benefits at any age, the majority of Social Security recipients—approximately 60%—receive Social Security retirement benefits due to retirement.

Social security retirement benefits are generally not subject to income tax. A relatively small number of people in the higher income tax brackets may have to pay some tax on a fraction of their benefits.

Eligibility

The Social Security Administration has set age 65 as the retirement age for a person who was born before 1938 to receive full social security retirement benefits (known as "full retirement age"). Beginning in the year 2000, the age at which a person's full retirement benefits are payable will increase gradually to age 67. For example, those born in 1940 reach "full retirement age" at 65 and 6 months. Individuals born in 1950, reach full retirement age at 66. Anybody born in 1960 or later will not be eligible for full retirement benefits until age 67.

There are additional eligibility requirements for Social Security. For example, one must have worked for a specified number of years before becoming eligible to receive Social Security retirement benefits. The amount of one's monthly Social Security benefits is calculated according to a specified formula based on their average earnings over those employment years. The earnings are tracked according to one's Social Security number.

As an individual works and pays Social Security taxes, he or she earns Social Security "credits," up to a maximum of four credits per year. The amount of money needed to earn one credit goes up each year. Currently, most people need 40 credits to qualify for benefits. However, it is the income, not the number of credits one earns, that determines the amount of the benefit.

Supplemental Security Income

Individuals who haven't worked long enough to be eligible for Social Security, or whose benefits are very low, may be eligible to receive additional benefits under another government program entitled Supplemental Security Income (SSI). General tax revenues from the U.S. Treasury are used to finance the SSI program.

In order to be eligible for SSI payments, one's income and assets must fall below certain established limits. Not all assets are taken into account. For example, a home and personal belongings are not counted, but bank accounts and cash on hand are included in the calculation. Although SSI is a federal program, some states supplement the national payments, establish higher SSI rates, and allow higher income limits than others.

APPENDICES

APPENDIX 1:

LIFE EXPECTANCY TABLES, REMAINING YEARS OF LIFE BASED ON AGE, ALL RACES, 1996

AGE	BOTH SEXES	MALE	FEMALE
0	76.1	73.0	79.0
1	75.6	72.6	78.6
5	71.7	68.7	74.7
10	66.8	63.8	69.7
15	61.9	58.9	64.8
20	57.1	54.2	59.9
25	52.4	49.6	55.1
30	47.7	44.9	50.2
35	43.0	40.4	45.4
40	38.4	35.9	40.7
45	33.9	31.5	36.0
50	29.4	27.1	31.5
55	25.2	23.0	27.1
60	21.2	19.2	22.9
65	17.5	15.7	18.9
70	14.1	12.5	15.3
75	11.1	9.8	11.9
80	8.3	7.3	8.9
85	6.1	5.4	6.4

Source: United States Department of Health.

APPENDIX 2:

AVERAGE AMOUNT OF LIFE INSURANCE COVERAGE PER HOUSEHOLD CATEGORIZED BY STATE - 1995

STATE	AMOUNT
Alabama	$119,300
Alaska	124,700
Arizona	97,800
Arkansas	96,300
California	114,900
Colorado	131,800
Connecticut	188,400
Delaware	196,100
D.C.	271,700
Florida	102,700
Georgia	143,500
Hawaii	166,000
Idaho	101,900
Illinois	137,200
Indiana	116,800
Iowa	127,500
Kansas	133,200
Kentucky	93,200
Louisiana	107,900
Maine	99,900
Maryland	144,600
Massachusetts	140,800

STATE	AMOUNT
Michigan	120,600
Minnesota	137,200
Mississippi	99,100
Missouri	121,500
Montana	94,900
Nebraska	135,200
Nevada	89,900
New Hampshire	133,600
New Jersey	178,300
New Mexico	107,900
New York	136,100
North Carolina	126,500
North Dakota	124,800
Ohio	122,500
Oklahoma	91,800
Oregon	100,700
Pennsylvania	131,900
Rhode Island	142,400
South Carolina	121,200
South Dakota	118,900
Tennessee	115,400
Texas	119,400
Utah	121,000
Vermont	122,300
Virginia	139,800

STATE	AMOUNT
Washington	100,100
West Virginia	80,400
Wisconsin	114,100
Wyoming	103,500

Source: American Council of Life Insurance and U.S. Bureau of the Census.

APPENDIX 3:

FIFTY TOP-RATED LIFE/HEALTH INSURANCE COMPANIES ACCORDING TO WARD'S FINANCIAL GROUP

COMPANY NAME (listed alphabetically)

AFLAC

Alfa Life Insurance Corp.

Allianz Life Insurance Co. of North America

American General Life and Accident Insurance Co.

American Life Insurance Co.

American National Insurance Co.

Ameritas Life Insurance Corp.

Bankers Life & Casualty Co.

Beneficial Life Insurance Co.

Cincinnati Life Insurance Co.

Country Life Insurance Co.

Employers Health Insurance Co.

Farm Bureau Life Insurance Co.

Farm Bureau Life Insurance Co. of Michigan

Federated Life Insurance Co.

First Colony Life Insurance Co.

Fortis Benefits Insurance Co.

General American Life Insurance Co.

Golden Rule Insurance Co.

Great American Life Insurance Co.

Guardian Life Insurance Co. of America

Horace Mann Life Insurance Co.

IDS Life Insurance Co.

Jackson National Life Insurance Co.

Jefferson-Pilot Life Insurance Co.

John Hancock Mutual Life Insurance Co.

Liberty National Life Insurance Co.

Midland National Life Insurance Co.

Minnesota Mutual Life Insurance Co.

Mutual of Omaha Insurance Co.

New York Life Insurance Co.

Northwestern Mutual Life Insurance Co.

Ohio National Life Insurance Co.

Pacific Mutual Life Insurance Co.

Primerica Life Insurance Co.

Physicians Mutual Insurance Co.

Provident Mutual Life Insurance Co.

Principal Mutual Life Insurance Co.

SAFECO Life Insurance Co.

ReliaStar Life Insurance Co.

Southern Farm Bureau Life Insurance Co.

Sentry Life Insurance Co.

Teachers Insurance and Annuity Association of America (TIAA)

SunAmerica Life Insurance Co.

Trustmark Insurance Co.

Transamerica Occidental Life Insurance Co.

UNUM Life Insurance Co. of America

United Insurance Co. of America

Western & Southern Life Insurance Co.

USAA Life Insurance Co.

APPENDIX 4:

LIFE INSURANCE OWNERSHIP ASSIGNMENT

______________________________________("Policy Owner")

and__________________________________("Transferee") hereby agree as follows:

Policy Owner is the owner of a life insurance policy more fully described as follows: (Describe policy in full detail, including name of company, policy number, etc.).

Policy Owner desires to assign said policy to Transferee as Transferee's sole property.

If there was any consideration or payment by the Transferee to the Policy Owner for the assignment of ownership, describe the consideration paid.

Policy Owner hereby releases and waives all rights to, or incidents of ownership in, the above described insurance policy, including but not limited to:

a) the right to name beneficiaries and to change any existing beneficiaries of the policy;

b) the right to make all payments required by the policy;

c) the right to surrender, cancel or convert the policy.

Dated: *Insert date.*

By:

Name of Policy Owner

By:

Name of Transferee

Notary Stamp

APPENDIX 5:

FORTY TOP-RATED ANNUITY COMPANIES ACCORDING TO STANDARD & POOR

RANK	GROUP	LARGEST ANNUITY UNDERWRITER	RATING
1	Hartford Insurance Group	ITT Hartford Life & Annuity	AA
2	Nationwide Group	Nationwide Life Insurance Co.	AA+
3	Metropolitan Group	Metropolitan Life Insurance Co.	AA
4	Principal Financial Group	Principal Mutual Life Insurance Co.	AA+
5	Aetna Life & Health Group	Aetna Life Insurance & Annuity Co.	AA
6	Lincoln National Group	Lincoln National Life Insurance Co.	AA
7	Prudential of America Group	Prudential Insurance Co. of America	A+
8	CIGNA Group	Connecticut General Life Insurance Co.	AA
9	Aegon Group	AUSA Life Insurance Co.	AAA
10	American General Group	Variable Annuity Life Insurance Co.	AA+
11	AXA Insurance Group	Equitable Life Assurance Society of the U.S.	AA
12	John Hancock Group	John Hancock Mutual Life Insurance Co.	AA+
13	Jackson National Group	Jackson National Life Insurance Co.	AA
14	New York Life Group	New York Life Insurance Co.	AA+
15	Sunamerica Group	Anchor National Life Insurance Co.	AA
16	TIAA Family of Companies	Teachers Insurance & Annuity Association	AAA
17	ING Group	Security Life of Denver Insurance Co.	AA

RANK	GROUP	LARGEST ANNUITY UNDERWRITER	RATING
18	American Express Group	IDS Life Insurance Co.	Aapi
19	Manulife Financial Group	North American Security Life Insurance Co.	AA+
20	General American Group	General American Life Insurance Co.	AA-
21	Skandia Group	American Skandia Life Assurance Corp.	A
22	Mass Mutual Life Insurance Group	Massachusetts Mutual Life Insurance Co.	AAA
23	Allstate Insurance Group	Northbrook Life Insurance Co.	AA+
24	Pacific Mutual Life Group	Pacific Mutual Life Insurance Co.	AA+
25	Travelers Insurance Group	Travelers Insurance Co. Life Dept.	AA-
26	American International Group	American Life Insurance Co.	AAA
27	General Electric Group	Life Insurance Co. of Virginia	AA
28	Transamerica Group	Transamerica Life Insurance & Annuity Co.	AA
29	Allmerica Financial Group	Allmerica Financial Life & Annuity	AA-
30	Great West Life Assurance Group	Great-West Life & Annuity Insurance Co.	AA+
31	Sun Life Assurance of Canada Group	Sun Life Assurance Co. of Canada (U.S.)	AAA
32	Allianz Insurance Group	Allianz Life Insurance Co. North America	Api
33	Reliastar Life Insurance Group	Northern Life Insurance Co.	AA-
34	Liberty Mutual Insurance Group	Keyport Life Insurance Co.	AA
35	Conseco Group	American Life & Casualty Insurance Co.	A+
36	Safeco Insurance Group	Safeco Life Insurance Co.	AA

RANK	GROUP	LARGEST ANNUITY UNDERWRITER	RATING
37	ARM Financial Group	Integrity Life Insurance Co.	A
38	Mutual of Omaha Group	United of Omaha Life Insurance Co.	AA
39	Merrill Lynch Group	Merrill Lynch Life Insurance Co.	AA
40	CNA Insurance Group	Continental Assurance Co.	AA-

Source: Insurance News Network.

APPENDIX 6:

HEALTH PLAN COMPARISON CHART

TYPE OF PLAN	FEATURES
FFS	Indemnity coverage, pays for "reasonable and customary" medical expenses, highest premiums, most flexibility in choosing health care providers, usually does not cover preventive care
PPO	Managed care, less out-of-pocket expense and paperwork if you go to an in-network provider, lower premiums, financial incentive to stay with selected providers, some preventive care covered
POS	Managed care, less out-of-pocket expense and paperwork if you stay in network and get referrals from your primary care physician, lower premiums, more financial incentive with the added restriction of the primary care physician, more preventive care measures
HMO	Managed care, pays only for visits to in-network providers, lowest premiums, no coverage if you go outside of network, most comprehensive preventive care measures

Source: Insurance News Network.

APPENDIX 7:

DIRECTORY OF STATE OFFICES OF LONG-TERM CARE OMBUSDSMAN

STATE	DEPARTMENT	ADDRESS	TELEPHONE NUMBER
Alabama	Commission on Aging	136 Catoma Street, 2nd Floor, Montgomery, AL 36130	205-242-5743
Alaska	Office of the Older Alaskans Ombudsman	3601 C Street, Suite 260, Anchorage, AK 99503	907-279-2232
Arizona	Aging and Adult Administration	1400 West Washington Street, Phoenix, AZ 85005	602-542-4446
Arkansas	Arkansas State Office on Aging	1417 Donaghey Plaza South, Little Rock, AR 72203	501-682-8952
California	Department of Aging	1600 K Street, Sacramento, CA 95814	916-322-6681
Colorado	Aging and Adult Services Division	455 Sherman Street, Denver, CO 80203	303-722-0300
Connecticut	Department on Aging	175 Main Street, Hartford, CT 06106	203-566-7770
Delaware	Division of Aging	1113 Church Avenue, Milford, DE 19963	302-422-1386
District of Columbia	Office on Aging	1909 K Street N.W., Washington, DC 20049	202-833-6720
Florida	Program Office of Aging and Adult Services	154 Holland Avenue, Tallahassee, FL 32399	904-488-6190
Georgia	Office of Aging	878 Peachtree Street N.E., Room 632, Atlanta, GA 30309	404-894-5336
Hawaii	Executive Office on Aging	335 Merchant Street, Room 241, Honolulu, HI 96813	808-548-2539
Idaho	Office on Aging	State House, Room 114, Boise, ID 83720	208-334-3833
Illinois	Department on Aging	421 East Capitol Avenue, Springfield, IL 62706	217-785-3140

STATE	DEPARTMENT	ADDRESS	TELEPHONE NUMBER
Indiana	Department on Aging & Community Services	251 N. Illinois Street, Indianapolis, IN 46204	317-232-7020
Iowa	Commission on Aging	914 Grand Avenue, Suite 236, Jewett Building, Des Moines, IA 50319	515-281-5187
Kansas	Department of Aging	915 Southwest Harrison, Topeka, KS 66612	913-296-4986
Kentucky	Division for Aging Services	275 East Main Street, 6th Floor, Frankfort, KY 40601	502-564-6930
Louisiana	Office of Elderly Affairs	4528 Bennington Avenue, LA 70898	504-925-1700
Maine	Commission on Aging	State House, Station No. 127, Augusta, ME 04333	207-289-3658
Maryland	Office on Aging	301 West Preston Street, Baltimore, MD 21201	301-225-1083
Massachusetts	Department of Elder Affairs	38 Chauncy Street, Boston, MA 02111	617-727-7273
Michigan	Citizens for Better Care	1627 East Kalamazoo, Lansing, MI 48912	517-482-1297
Minnesota	Office of Ombudsman for Older Minnesotans	444 Lafayette Road, St. Paul, MN 55155	612-296-3969
Mississippi	Mississippi Council on Aging	421 West Pascagoula Street, Jackson, MS 39203	601-949-2070
Missouri	Division on Aging	2701 West Main Street, Jefferson City, MO 65102	314-751-3082
Montana	Seniors' Office of Legal and Ombudsman Services,	P.O. Box 232, Capitol Station, Helena, MT 59620	406-444-4676
Nebraska	Department on Aging	301 Centennial Mall South, Lincoln, NE 68509	402-471-2306
Nevada	Division of Aging Services	340 North 11th Street, Suite 114, Las Vegas, NV 89101	702-486-3545

STATE	DEPARTMENT	ADDRESS	TELEPHONE NUMBER
New Hampshire	Division of Elderly and Adult Services	6 Hazen Drive, Concord, NH 03301	603-271-4375
New Jersey	Office of the Ombudsman for the Institutionalized Elderly	28 West State Street, Room 305, Trenton, NJ 08625	609-292-8016
New Mexico	State Agency on Aging	224 East Palace Avenue, 4th Floor, Santa Fe, NM 87501	505-827-7640
New York	Office for the Aging	Empire State Plaza, Agency Building No. 2, Albany, NY 12223	518-474-7329
North Carolina	Division of Aging	693 Palmer Drive, Raleigh, NC 27603	919-733-8400
North Dakota	Aging Services	State Capitol Building, Bismarck, ND 58505	701-224-2577
Ohio	Department of Aging	50 West Broad Street, 9th Floor, Columbus, OH 43215	614-466-9927
Oklahoma	Special Unit on Aging	P.O. Box 25352, Oklahoma City, OK 73125	405-521-6734
Oregon	Office of Long-Term Care Ombudsman	2475 Lancaster Drive, Building B, Number 9, Salem, OR 97310	503-378-6533
Pennsylvania	Department of Aging	231 State Street, Harrisburg, PA 17120	717-783-7247
Rhode Island	Department of Elderly Affairs	160 Pine Street, Providence, RI 02903	401-277-6883
South Carolina	Division of Ombudsman and Citizens' Service	1205 Pendleton Street, Columbia, SC 29201	803-734-0457
South Dakota	Office of Adult Services and Aging	700 North Illinois Street, Pierre, SD 57501	605-773-3656
Tennessee	Commission on Aging	706 Church Street, Suite 201, Nashville, TN 37243	615-741-2056
Texas	Department on Aging	P.O. Box 12786, Capitol Station, Austin, TX 78741	512-444-2727

STATE	DEPARTMENT	ADDRESS	TELEPHONE NUMBER
Utah	Division of Aging and Adult Services	120 North - 200 West, Box 45500, Salt Lake City, UT 84145	801-538-3924
Vermont	Office on Aging	103 South Main Street, Waterbury, VT 05676	02-241-2400
Virginia	Office on Aging	700 East Frannklin Street, Richmond, VA 23219	804-225-2271
Washington	South King County Multi-Service Center	1200 South 336 Street, Federal Way, Olympia, WA 98003	206-838-6810
West Virginia	Commission on Aging	State Capitol, Charleston, WV 25305	304-558-3317
Wisconsin	Board on Aging and Long Term Care	214 North Hamilton Street, Madison, WI 53703	608-266-8944
Wyoming	State Bar Association	900 8th Street, Wheatland, WY 82201	307-322-5553

APPENDIX 8:

STATE AUTOMOBILE INSURANCE MINIMUM MONETARY LIABILITY CHART

STATE	AMOUNT (In Thousands of Dollars)
Alabama	20/40/10
Alaska	50/100/25
Arizona	15/30/10
Arkansas	25/50/15
California	15/30/5
Colorado	25/50/15
Connecticut	20/40/10
Delaware	15/30/10
D.C.	25/50/10
Florida	10/20/10
Georgia	15/30/10
Hawaii	35/15/10
Idaho	25/50/15
Illinois	20/40/15
Indiana	25/50/10
Iowa	20/40/15
Kansas	25/50/10
Kentucky	25/50/10
Louisiana	10/20/10
Maine	20/40/10
Maryland	20/40/10
Massachusetts	20/40/8

STATE	AMOUNT (In Thousands of Dollars)
Michigan	20/40/10
Minnesota	30/60/10
Mississippi	10/20/05
Missouri	25/50/10
Montana	25/50/10
Nebraska	25/50/25
Nevada	15/30/10
New Hampshire	25/50/25
New Jersey	15/30/5
New Mexico	25/50/10
New York	25/50/10*
North Carolina	25/50/15
North Dakota	25/50/25
Ohio	12.5/25/7.5
Oklahoma	10/20/10
Oregon	25/50/10
Pennsylvania	15/30/5
Rhode Island	25/50/25
South Carolina	15/30/5
South Dakota	25/50/25
Tennessee	20/50/10
Texas	20/40/15
Utah	25/50/15
Vermont	20/40/10
Virginia	25/50/20

STATE	AMOUNT (In Thousands of Dollars)
Washington	25/50/10
West Virginia	20/40/10
Wisconsin	25/50/10
Wyoming	25/50/20

Note: The first number denotes the bodily injury liability maximum for one person injured in an accident; the second number denotes the bodily injury maximum for all injuries in one accident; the third number denotes the property damage liability maximum for one accident;

* liability raised to 50/100 if death occurs.

Source: Insurance Information Institute Property and Casualty Fact Book, 1997.

APPENDIX 9:

DIRECTORY OF STATE INSURANCE DEPARTMENTS

STATE	DEPARTMENT	ADDRESS	TELEPHONE NUMBER
Alabama	Department of Insurance	201 Monroe Street, Suite 1700, Montgomery, Alabama 36104	334-269-3550
Alaska	Division of Insurance	State Office Building, 333 Willoughby Avenue, 9th Floor, P.O. Box 110805, Juneau, Alaska 99811-0805	907-465-2515
Arizona	Department of Insurance	2910 N. 44Th Street, Suite 210, Phoenix, Arizona 85018	602-912-4444
Arkansas	Department of Insurance	1200 West 3rd Street, Little Rock, Arkansas 72201-1904	501-371-2600
California	Department of Insurance	300 Capital Mall, Suite 1500, Sacramento, California 95814	8213-897-8921
Colorado	Division of Insurance	1560 Broadway, Suite 850, Denver, Colorado 80202	303-894-7499
Connecticut	Insurance Department	P.O. Box 816, Hartford, Connecticut 06142-0816	860-297-3802
Delaware	Department of Insurance	1st Federal Plaza, 710 North King Street, Wilmington, Delaware 19801	302-577-3119
District of Columbia	Department of Insurance	441 Fourth St. NW, 8th Floor North, Washington, DC 20001	202-727-8000
Florida	Department of Insurance	9000 Regency Square Boulevard, Suite 201, Jacksonville, Florida 32211	904-727-5505

STATE	DEPARTMENT	ADDRESS	TELEPHONE NUMBER
Georgia	Office of Commissioner of Insurance	2 Martin Luther King, Jr. Drive, Atlanta, Georgia 30334	404-656-2056
Hawaii	Insurance Commissioner's Office,	250 S. King Street, Honolulu, Hawaii 96813	808-586-2790
Idaho	Department of Insurance	700 West State Street, Boise, Idaho 83720-0043	208-334-4250
Illinois	Department of Insurance	320 West Washington Street, 4th Floor, Springfield, Illinois 62767	217-782-4515
Indiana	Department of Insurance	311 West Washington Street, Suite 300, Indianapolis, Indiana 46204-2787	317-232-2385
Iowa	Insurance Division	Lucas Building, 6th Floor, Des Moines, Iowa 50319	515-281-5705
Kansas	Insurance Department	420 S.W. Ninth Street, Topeka, Kansas 66612-1678	913-296-7801
Kentucky	Department of Insurance	215 West Main Street, Frankfort, Kentucky 40601	502-564-3630
Louisiana	Department of Insurance	950 North Fifth Street, Baton Rouge, Louisiana 70804-9214	504-342-5900
Maine	Bureau of Insurance	34 State House Station, Augusta, Maine 04333	207-624-8475
Maryland	Insurance Administration	525 St. Paul Place, Baltimore, Maryland 21202	410-468-2000
Massachusetts	Division of Insurance	470 Atlantic Avenue, 6th Floor, Boston, Massachusetts 02110-2223	617-521-7794
Michigan	Insurance Bureau	611 West Ottawa Street, 2nd Floor North, Lansing, Michigan 48933	517-373-9273
Minnesota	Division of Insurance	133 East 7th Street, St. Paul, Minnesota 55101	612-296-6848

STATE	DEPARTMENT	ADDRESS	TELEPHONE NUMBER
Mississippi	Department of Insurance	1804 Walter Sillers Building, Jackson, Mississippi 39201	601-359-3569
Missouri	Department of Insurance	P.O. Box 690, Jefferson City, Missouri 65102-0690	573-751-2640
Montana	Department of Insurance	126 North Sanders, Room 270, Helena, Montana 59620	406-444-2040
Nebraska	Department of Insurance	941 O Street, Suite 400, Lincoln, Nebraska 68508-3690	402-471-2201
Nevada	Department of Insurance	1665 Hot Springs Road, Suite 152, Carson City, Nevada 89710	702-687-7650
New Hampshire	Insurance Department	169 Manchester Street, Suite 1, Concord, New Hampshire 03301-5151	603-271-2261
New Jersey	Department of Insurance	20 West State Street, CN325, Trenton, New Jersey 08625-0325	609-292-5363
New Mexico	Insurance Division	P.O. Drawer 1269, Santa Fe, New Mexico 87504-1269	505-827-4601
New York	Insurance Department	Empire State Plaza, Agency Building No. 1, Albany, New York 12257	518-474-6600
North Carolina	Department of Insurance	P.O. Box 26387, Raleigh, North Carolina 27611	919-733-7343
North Dakota	Department of Insurance	600 East Boulevard, Bismarck, North Dakota 58505-0320	701-328-2440
Ohio	Department of Insurance	2100 Stella Court, Columbus, Ohio 43215-1067	614-644-2658

STATE	DEPARTMENT	ADDRESS	TELEPHONE NUMBER
Oklahoma	Department of Insurance	3814 N. Santa Fe, Oklahoma City, Oklahoma 73118	405-521-2686
Oregon	Insurance Division	350 Winter St. NE, Room 200, Salem, Oregon 97310-0200	503-947-7980
Pennsylvania	Department of Insurance	1326 Strawberry Square, Harrisburg, Pennsylvania 17120	717-787-2317
Rhode Island	Insurance Department	233 Richmond Street, Suite 233, Providence, Rhode Island 02903-4233	401-277-2223
South Carolina	Department of Insurance	P.O. Box 100105, Columbia, South Carolina 29202-3105	803-737-6150
South Dakota	Insurance Division	500 East Capitol, Pierre, South Dakota 57501-5070	605-773-3563
Tennessee	Department of Insurance	500 James Robertson Parkway, Nashville, Tennessee 37243-0565	615-741-2241
Texas	Department of Insurance	P.O. Box 149104, Austin, Texas 78714-9104	512-463-6464
Utah	Insurance Department	3110 State Office Building, Salt Lake City, Utah 84114	801-538-3800
Vermont	Insurance Division	89 Main Street, Drawer 20, Montpelier, Vermont 05620-3101	802-828-3301
Virginia	Bureau of Insurance	P.O. Box 1157, Richmond, Virginia 23218	800-552-7945
Washington	Office of Insurance Commissioner	P.O. Box 40255, Olympia, Washington 98504-0255	360-753-7301
West Virginia	Insurance Department	P.O. Box 50540, Charleston, West Virginia 25305-0540	304-558-3354

STATE	DEPARTMENT	ADDRESS	TELEPHONE NUMBER
Wisconsin	Office of the Commissioner of Insurance	121 East Wilson Street, Madison, Wisconsin 53702	608-266-3585
Wyoming	Insurance Department	122 West 25th Street, 3rd Floor East, Cheyenne, Wyoming 82002-0440	307-777-7401

APPENDIX 10:

DIRECTORY OF MAJOR CASUALTY AND PROPERTY INSURANCE COMPANIES

COMPANY	TELEPHONE	INSURANCE CODE
Aetna Insurance Co. of Connecticut	(860) 277-0111	050
AIU Insurance Co.	(888) 244-2736	267
Allied Mutual Insurance Co.	(800) 282-9445	N/A
Allstate Insurance Co.	(800) 386-6126	011
Amco Insurance Co.	(800) 282-9445	N/C
American Casualty Co.	(800) 437-8854	015
American Economy Insurance Co.	(317) 262-6262	053
American Employers Insurance Co.	(617) 725-7033	022
American Family Mutual Insurance Co.	(800) 374-1111	N/A
American Home Assurance Co.	(888) 244-2736	027
American International Ins. Co.	(800) 562-2208	N/A
American States Insurance Co.	(317) 262-6262	054
Anthem Casualty Insurance Co.	(800) 537-5568	N/A
Arbella Mutual Insurance Co.	(617) 328-2428	N/A
Arkwright Mutual Insurance Co.	(781) 890-9300	N/A
Atlanta Casualty Co.	(770) 447-8930	N/A
Atlantic Mutual Insurance Co.	(800) 945-7461	045
Atlas Assurance Co. of America	(609) 888-1300	N/A
Auto-Owners Insurance Co.	(517) 323-1365	N/A
Birmingham Fire Insurance of Pennsylvania	(888) 244-2736	N/A
Buckeye Union Insurance Co.	(800) 669-6076	439
California State Auto Assn.	(415) 563-0828	N/A
Camden Fire Insurance Assn.	(888) 421-2111	073

COMPANY	TELEPHONE	INSURANCE CODE
CIGNA Property & Casualty Ins Co.	(215) 761-1000	004
Citizens Insurance Co. of America	(800) 628-0250	648
Commerce & Industry Insurance Co.	(888) 244-2736	087
Commercial Union Insurance Co.	(617) 725-7033	089
Continental Casualty Co.	(800) 669-6076	097
Continental Insurance Co.	(800) 669-6076	098
Coregis Insurance Co.	(312) 849-5000	N/A
Cumis Insurance Society Inc.	(800) 637-2676	448
Dairyland Insurance Co.	(715) 346-9200	N/A
DeSoto Insurance Co.	(888) 823-9754	N/A
Federal Insurance Co.	(212) 483-4399	124
Fidelity & Deposit Co. of Maryland	(800) 854-6011	N/A
Fire Insurance Exchange	(213) 964-8911	N/A
Firemens Insurance Co. of Newark, New Jersey	(800) 669-6076	132
Foremost Insurance Co.	(800) 527-3907	136
GEICO Indemnity Co.	(800) 848-6502	100
General Accident Ins. Co. of America	(888) 421-2111	622
General Casualty of Wisconsin	(608) 825-5715	N/A
General Insurance Co. of America	(206) 545-5841	140
Georgia Farm Bureau Mutual Ins Co.	(912) 474-8411	N/A
Globe Indemnity Co.	(800) 843-7925	147
Government Employees Insurance Co.	(800) 848-6502	148
Grange Mutual Casualty Co.	(614) 445-2625	N/A
Great American Insurance Co.	(800) 724-7722	154
Great West Casualty Co.	(800) 228-8040	N/A
Hanover Insurance Co.	(508) 855-8000	158

COMPANY	TELEPHONE	INSURANCE CODE
Hartford Accident & Indemnity Co.	(860) 547-4780	161
Hartford Casualty Insurance Co.	(860) 547-4780	N/A
Hartford Fire Insurance Co.	(860) 547-4780	162
Horace Mann Insurance Co.	(800) 999-1030	458
Insurance Co. of North America	(215) 761-1000	173
Insurance Co. of the State of Pennsylvania	(888) 244-2736	175
Integon National Insurance Co.	(800) 468-3466	N/A
Interinsurance Exchange Auto Club So.	(714) 850-5111	N/A
John Deere Insurance Co.	(800) 635-3377	480
Lexington Insurance Co.	(888) 244-2736	N/A
Liberty Insurance Corp.	(800) 526-1547	672
Liberty Mutual Fire Insurance Co.	(800) 526-1547	182
Liberty Mutual Insurance Co.	(800) 526-1547	183
Lumbermens Mutual Casualty Co.	(847) 320-2414	190
Medical Liability Mutual Ins Co.	(212) 576-9850	N/A
Mercury Insurance Co. of California	(213) 964-8911	N/A
Metropolitan Property & Casualty Co.	(800) 854-6011	211
Mid-Century Insurance Co.	(213) 964-8911	N/A
Motors Insurance Corp.	(313) 556-4632	677
National Fire Ins. Co. of Hartford	(800) 669-6076	224
National Indemnity Co.	(402) 536-3000	N/A
National Union Fire Ins.oOf Pittsburgh	(888) 244-2736	N/A
Nationwide Mutual Fire Insurance Co.	(800) 421-3535	230
Nationwide Mutual Insurance Co.	(800) 421-3535	231
New Hampshire Insurance Co.	(888) 244-2736	235
New Jersey Manufacturers Ins. Co.	(609) 883-1300	426

COMPANY	TELEPHONE	INSURANCE CODE
North Carolina Farm Bureau Mutual Ins.	(919) 782-1705	N/A
North River Insurance Co.	(800) 690-5520	250
Northern Assurance Co. of America	(617) 725-7033	N/A
Ohio Casualty Insurance Co.	(513) 867-3000	465
Pacific Employers Insurance Co.	(215) 761-1000	423
Pacific Indemnity Co.	(212) 483-4399	268
Phoenix Insurance Co.	(800) 252-4633	282
Preferred Risk Mutual Insurance Co.	(515) 267-5299	288
Progressive Casualty Insurance Co.	(800) 274-4499	413
Progressive Northern Insurance Co.	(800) 274-4499	413
Progressive Northwestern Ins. Co.	(800) 274-4499	413
Progressive Specialty Insurance Co.	(800) 274-4499	413
Protection Mutual Insurance Co.	(847) 825-4474	N/A
Reliance Insurance Co.	(215) 761-1000	N/A
Republic Underwriters Insurance Co.	(214) 559-1270	N/A
Royal Insurance Co. of America	(800) 843-7925	293
Safeco Insurance Co. of America	(206) 545-5841	304
Scottsdale Insurance Co.	(602) 948-0505	N/A
Selective Insurance Co. of America	(973) 948-2900	315
Sentry Insurance	(715) 346-9200	N/A
Shelter Mutual Insurance Co.	(800) 743-5837	N/A
Standard Fire Insurance Co.	(800) 252-4633	325
State Farm Fire & Casualty Co.	(800) 732-5246	327
State Farm Indemnity Co.	(800) 732-5246	N/A
State Farm Lloyds	(800) 732-5246	N/A
State Farm Mutual Automobile Ins. Co.	(800) 732-5246	328

COMPANY	TELEPHONE	INSURANCE CODE
Travelers Indemnity Co.	(860) 277-0111	344
Trinity Universal Insurance Co.	(214) 360-8039	N/A
United Services Automobile Assn.	(800) 531-8222	355
United States Fire Insurance Co.	(800) 690-5520	358
USAA Casualty Insurance Co.	(800) 531-8222	356
Utica Mutual Insurance Co.	(800) 695-1914	364
Vesta Fire Insurance Corp.	(800) 444-3928	N/A
Vigilant Insurance Co.	(212) 483-4399	368
Westfield Insurance Co.	(800) 443-3311	N/A
Zenith Insurance Co.	(800) 440-5020	N/A

Source: New York Lawyers Diary and Manual.

APPENDIX 11:

AVERAGE AUTOMOBILE INSURANCE PREMIUMS— BY STATE

STATE	AVERAGE PREMIUM EXPEN-DITURE	RANK	COMBINED	LIABILITY	COLLISION	COMPRE-HENSIVE
Alabama	$577.86	33	$661.60	$313.60	$246.04	$101.97
Alaska	$750.91	16	$904.05	$464.97	$308.83	$130.26
Arizona	$785.05	12	$869.11	$514.67	$208.00	$146.44
Arkansas	$557.70	34	$663.67	$331.12	$221.97	$110.58
California	$790.70	11	$904.56	$512.27	$254.93	$137.36
Colorado	$751.25	15	$854.87	$481.50	$197.64	$175.72
Connecticut	$899.27	5	$976.97	$605.23	$259.73	$112.01
Delaware	$806.05	8	$873.66	$568.57	$220.25	$84.84
District of Columbia	$993.07	2	$1,123.1	$576.46	$354.55	$192.18
Florida	$783.23	13	$823.61	$512.23	$204.53	$106.86
Georgia	$627.47	25	$761.34	$332.55	$299.54	$129.25
Hawaii	$958.69	4	$1,092.5	$726.32	$265.01	$101.24
Idaho	$464.56	47	$556.22	$284.36	$173.29	$98.57
Illinois	$637.98	24	$703.73	$363.09	$226.47	$114.17
Indiana	$548.06	38	$637.22	$335.41	$206.64	$95.16
Iowa	$445.39	50	$507.16	$255.55	$154.28	$97.33
Kansas	$495.26	43	$606.29	$271.31	$175.19	$159.79
Kentucky	$581.05	31	$697.99	$381.18	$223.08	$93.73
Louisiana	$802.17	10	$921.32	$543.35	$243.12	$134.86
Maine	$470.18	46	$538.13	$286.04	$177.90	$74.18
Maryland	$759.44	14	$817.89	$478.22	$229.75	$109.92
Massachu-setts	$832.83	7	$914.08	$588.22	$212.74	$113.11

STATE	AVERAGE PREMIUM EXPEN-DITURE	RANK	COMBINED	LIABILITY	COLLISION	COMPRE-HENSIVE
Michigan	$697.38	18	$834.64	$348.49	$346.92	$139.24
Minnesota	$653.98	23	$713.33	$437.10	$155.89	$120.34
Mississippi	$604.17	27	$706.40	$333.12	$244.45	$128.83
Missouri	$599.35	29	$681.20	$355.99	$210.15	$115.06
Montana	$478.96	44	$605.52	$275.93	$176.17	$153.43
Nebraska	$475.13	45	$572.91	$262.03	$161.53	$149.36
Nevada	$802.50	9	$912.96	$555.60	$236.97	$120.39
New Hampshire	$621.44	26	$681.30	$371.09	$232.38	$77.83
New Jersey	$1,099.0	1	$1,259.4	$726.86	$364.09	$168.47
New Mex-ico	$659.80	22	$812.03	$420.68	$235.18	$156.17
New York	$959.83	3	$1,113.2	$654.73	$265.40	$193.07
North Carolina	$518.28	41	$594.79	$350.75	$169.36	$74.69
North Dakota	$401.55	51	$505.97	$214.13	$151.33	$140.51
Ohio	$553.27	36	$609.67	$341.11	$189.58	$78.97
Oklahoma	$545.42	39	$670.87	$333.72	$183.79	$153.36
Oregon	$584.76	30	$660.76	$382.37	$186.57	$91.82
Pennsyl-vania	$687.43	19	$764.15	$443.57	$219.33	$101.25
Rhode Island	$869.50	6	$1,014.0	$615.83	$281.94	$116.28
South Carolina	$601.97	28	$698.30	$396.06	$198.43	$103.81
South Dakota	$448.33	49	$570.86	$261.01	$152.74	$157.10
Tennessee	$556.90	35	$637.68	$313.01	$231.89	$92.78

STATE	AVERAGE PREMIUM EXPEN- DITURE	RANK	COMBINED	LIABILITY	COLLISION	COMPRE- HENSIVE
Texas	$726.05	17	$820.38	$504.88	$176.91	$138.59
Utah	$580.72	32	$671.31	$370.31	$199.33	$101.66
Vermont	$514.17	42	$589.72	$292.10	$212.17	$85.45
Virginia	$549.67	37	$608.87	$358.32	$172.48	$78.07
Washington	$665.88	21	$732.72	$455.97	$177.48	$99.27
West Virginia	$671.25	20	$784.49	$433.37	$235.01	$116.12
Wisconsin	$533.49	40	$586.98	$315.65	$166.42	$104.91
Wyoming	$451.62	48	$590.71	$238.90	$181.56	$170.25

APPENDIX 12:

SUBROGATION AGREEMENT - NO-FAULT INSURANCE LAW

DATE:

TO:[Name and Address of Applicant]

RE:[Name of Policyholder and Policy Number; Date of Accident; Insurance Company File Number]

FROM: [Name of Insurer's Claim Representative; Insurance Company; Address; Phone Number]

Dear Applicant:

Kindly complete and return this agreement at once. Failure to do so may delay payment of your No-Fault benefits.

SUBROGATION AGREEMENT

To: [Name of Insurer] (hereinafter "Company")

The undersigned hereby declares that a bodily injury was sustained by [name of applicant] on [date of accident] and a claim for extended economic loss benefits, including medical, loss of earnings, and other reasonable and necessary expenses and/or a death benefit, is being made under Policy Number [number] issued to [name of insured].

In consideration for benefits paid or payable under the additional personal injury protection endorsement of the foregoing policy, it is agreed that:

1. In accordance with the provisions of the policy, the Company is subrogated to the extent of any payment for additional first-party benefits to the rights of the applicant against any person who may be liable to the injured person because of bodily injury with respect to which additional personal injury protection benefits are afforded under this policy.

2. The undersigned shall cooperate with the Company and upon the Company's request, assist in the conduct of suits and in enforcing any Company right of subrogation for additional personal injury protection benefits paid against any person who may be liable to the injured person because of bodily injury with respect to which additional personal injury protection benefits are afforded under this policy.

3. The undersigned to or for whom payments are made or the undersigned's legal representative will notify the Company in writing prior to in-

stitution of any legal proceedings against any person legally responsible for the above described bodily injury and will do whatever is necessary to secure and to do nothing to prejudice the Company's subrogation rights.

I have carefully read the foregoing subrogation agreement, understand its contents, and have signed the same as my free act.

Date: ___________

____

BY: [Signature of Applicant]

APPENDIX 13:

SAMPLE COMPLAINT TO RECOVER NO-FAULT INSURANCE BENEFITS

[NAME OF COURT] **COMPLAINT**

[CAPTION OF CASE] **INDEX NO.**

The plaintiff, complaining of the defendant, by his attorney, [name of attorney], herein states the following:

1. Upon information and belief, the defendant is a foreign insurance corporation doing business in the State of___________, under the laws of the State of ___________.

2. At all times hereinafter mentioned, the defendant was and still is engaged in the business of insuring automobiles and the drivers thereof against certain hazards, including personal injuries.

3. On [date] the defendant issued and delivered an insurance policy, Policy No.___, to its insured, [name of insured].

4. Said insurance policy contains an agreement to insure the driver of the insured vehicle for "Basic Economic Loss" as described in Insurance Law § 5102(a), up to the limit set forth in the policy.

5. On or about [date of accident], at about [time of accident], and while the policy was in full force and effect, the plaintiff was injured while driving the insured vehicle with the permission of the insured, [name of insured].

6. Solely as a result of the accident and injuries sustained, the plaintiff suffered "Basic Economic Loss," hereinafter referred to as "First Party Benefits."

7. The plaintiff and/or the insured gave notice to the defendant as soon as practicable after the aforementioned accident.

8. On or about [date], some (#) months after the accident, the defendant sent a letter enclosing a copy of its No-Fault application form to the plaintiff.

9. The plaintiff has completed and properly executed all the forms supplied by the defendant and has submitted the required proof of his claim therewith.

10. Demand has been made of the defendant by the plaintiff for "First Party Benefits" and the defendant has not paid the sum or any part thereof.

11. More than thirty (30) days have elapsed since the accident and since the date of plaintiffs demand. Payments are therefore overdue.

12. That as a result of the above, the plaintiff incurred an uncompensated loss of wages, medical bills, interest, attorneys' fees and was otherwise injured and damaged in the sum of ________________ ($__________) Dollars.

WHEREFORE, plaintiff demands judgment against the defendant in the sum of ________________ ($__________) Dollars, plus interest, the costs and disbursements of this action, and such other and further relief as the Court deems just and proper.

[Name of Attorney]

Attorney for Plaintiff

[Attorney's Address]

[Attorney's Telephone Number]

Source: McKinney's Selected Consolidated Laws Forms, Volume 26A, West Publishing Company, 1992.

APPENDIX 14:

THE AUTO CHOICE REFORM ACT OF 1997 (S. 625 and HR. 2010)

Be it enacted by the Senate and House of Representatives of the United States of America in Congress assembled,

SECTION 1. SHORT TITLE.

This Act may be cited as the 'Auto Choice Reform Act of 1997'.

SECTION 2. FINDINGS.

Congress finds that—

(1) the costs of operating a motor vehicle are excessive due in substantial part to the legal and administrative costs associated with the resolution of claims under the tort liability insurance system;

(2) the tort liability insurance system often results in—

(A) the failure to provide compensation commensurate with loss;

(B) an unreasonable delay in the payment of benefits; and

(C) the expenditure of an excessive amount for legal fees;

(3) the incentives of the tort liability insurance system for motor vehicles are distorted, and result in—

(A) significant fraud in the claims process, which exacerbates the level of distrust of many individuals in the United States with respect to the legal process and the Xrule of law;

(B) significant, wasteful, fraudulent, and costly overuse and abuse of scarce health care resources and services;

(C) unbearable cost burdens on low-income individuals, imposing on them the Hobson's choice of driving on an unlawful, uninsured basis or foregoing essential needs, such as food and adequate shelter;

(D) significant reductions in, access to, and purchases of, motor vehicles, which—

(i) damage the economic well-being of many low-income individuals; and

(ii) cause unnecessary harm to a critical component of the economy of the United States;

(E) significant deterioration of the economic well-being of the majority of major cities in the United States through the imposition of a massive tort tax that—

(i) places a disproportionate burden on urban residents; and

(ii) contributes to the abandonment of the cities by many taxpayers who are able to achieve substantial after-tax savings on automobile insurance premiums by moving to adjacent suburban communities; and

(F) significant inability to achieve market-based discounts in insurance rates for owners of safer cars, which reduces the level of safety for drivers and passengers of motor vehicles;

(4) insurance to indemnify individuals for personal injuries arising from motor vehicle collisions is frequently unavailable at a reasonable cost because of the potential liability for third-party tort claims;

(5) a system that gives consumers the opportunity to insure themselves and that separates economic and noneconomic damages for the purposes of purchasing insurance would provide significant cost savings to drivers of motor vehicles;

(6) a system that enables individuals to choose the form of motor vehicle insurance that best suits their needs would—

(A) enhance individual freedom;

(B) reduce the cost of motor vehicle insurance; and

(C) increase average compensation in the event of an accident; and

(7) a system that targets and emphasizes the scourge of those individuals who drive under the influence of drugs or alcohol will further deter such dangerous and unlawful conduct.

SECTION 3. PURPOSE.

The purpose of this Act is to allow consumers of motor vehicle insurance to choose between—

(1) an insurance system that provides substantially the same remedies as are available under applicable State law; and

(2) a predominately first-party insurance system that provides for—

(A) more comprehensive recovery of economic loss in a shorter period of time; and

(B) the right to sue negligent drivers for any uncompensated economic losses.

SECTION 4. DEFINITIONS.

In this Act:

(1) Accident: The term 'accident' means an unforeseen or unplanned event that—

(A) causes loss or injury; and

(B) arises from the operation, maintenance, or use of a motor vehicle.

(2) Add-on law: The term 'add-on law' means a State law that provides that persons injured in motor vehicle accidents—

(A) are compensated without regard to fault for economic loss; and

(B) have the right to claim without any limitation for noneconomic loss based on fault.

(3) Economic loss: The term 'economic loss' means any objectively verifiable pecuniary loss resulting from an accident, including—

(A) reasonable and necessary medical and rehabilitation expenses;

(B) loss of earnings;

(C) burial costs;

(D) replacement services loss;

(E) costs of making reasonable accommodations to a personal residence to make the residence more habitable for an injured individual; and

(F) loss of employment, and loss of business or employment opportunities, to the extent recovery for such losses is allowed under applicable State law.

(4) Financial responsibility law: The term 'financial responsibility law' means a law (including a law requiring compulsory coverage) penalizing motorists for failing to carry defined limits of tort liability insurance covering motor vehicle accidents.

(5) Injury: The term 'injury' means bodily injury, sickness, disease, or death.

(6) Insurer: The term 'insurer' means—

(A) any person who is engaged in the business of issuing or delivering motor vehicle insurance policies (including aninsurance agent); or

(B) any person who is self-insured within the meaning of applicable State law.

(7) Intentional misconduct:

(A) In general: Except as provided in subparagraph (B), the term 'intentional misconduct' means conduct—

(i) with respect to which harm is intentionally caused or attempted to be caused by a person who acts or fails to act for the purpose of causing harm, or with knowledge that harm is substantially certain to result from that action or failure to act; and

(ii) that causes or substantially contributes to the harm that is the subject of a claim.

(B) Clarification: For purposes of this paragraph, a person does not intentionally cause or attempt to cause harm—

(i) solely because that person acts or fails to act with the understanding that the action or failure to act creates a grave risk of causing harm; or

(ii) if the act or omission by that person causing bodily harm is for the purpose of averting bodily harm to that person or another person.

(8) Motor vehicle: The term 'motor vehicle' means a vehicle of any kind required to be registered under the provisions of the applicable State law relating to motor vehicles.

(9) No-fault motor vehicle law: The term 'no-fault motor vehicle law' means a State law that provides that—

(A) persons injured in motor vehicle accidents are paid compensation without regard to fault for their economic loss that results from injury; and

(B) in return for the payment referred to in subparagraph (A), claims based on fault including claims for noneconomic loss, are limited to a defined extent.

(10) Noneconomic loss: The term 'noneconomic loss' means subjective, nonmonetary losses including pain, suffering, inconvenience, men-

tal suffering, emotional distress, loss of society and companionship, loss of consortium, hedonic damages, injury to reputation, and humiliation.

(11) Occupy: The term 'occupy' means, with respect to the operation, maintenance, or use of a motor vehicle, to be in or on a motor vehicle or to be engaged in the immediate act of entering into or alighting from a motor vehicle before or after its use for transportation.

(12) Operation, maintenance, or use of a motor vehicle:

(A) In general: The term 'operation, maintenance, or use of a motor vehicle' means occupying a motor vehicle.

(B) Exclusions: The term 'operation, maintenance, or use of a motor vehicle' does not include—

(i) conduct within the course of a business of manufacturing, sale, repairing, servicing, or otherwise maintaining motor vehicles, unless the conduct occurs outside of the scope of the business activity; or

(ii) conduct within the course of loading or unloading a motor vehicle, unless the conduct occurs while occupying the motor vehicle.

(13) Person: The term 'person' means any individual, corporation, company, association, firm, partnership, society, joint stock company, or any other entity, including any governmental entity.

(14) Personal protection insurance: The term 'personal protection insurance' means insurance that provides for—

(A) benefits to an insured person for economic loss without regard to fault for injury resulting from a motor vehicle accident; and

(B) a waiver of tort claims in accordance with this Act.

(15) Replacement services loss: The term 'replacement services loss' means expenses reasonably incurred in obtaining ordinary and necessary services from other persons who are not members of the injured person's household, in lieu of the services the injured person would have performed for the benefit of the household.

(16) Resident relative or dependent: The term 'resident relative or dependent' means a person who—

(A) is related to the owner of a motor vehicle by blood, marriage, adoption, or otherwise (including a dependent receiving financial services or support from such owner); and

(B)(i) resides in the same household as the owner of the motor vehicle at the time of the accident; or

(ii) usually makes a home in the same family unit as that owner, even though that person may temporarily live elsewhere.

(17) State: The term 'State' means any State of the United States, the District of Columbia, the Commonwealth of Puerto Rico, Guam, the United States Virgin Islands, American Samoa, the Commonwealth of the Northern Mariana Islands, the Trust Territories of the Pacific Islands, and any other territory or possession of the United States.

(18) Tort liability: The term 'tort liability' means the legal obligation to pay damages for an injury adjudged to have been committed by a tortfeasor.

(19) Tort liability insurance: The term 'tort liability insurance' means a contract of insurance under which an insurer agrees to pay, on behalf of an insured, damages that the insured is obligated to pay to a third person because of the liability of the insured to that person.

(20) Tort maintenance coverage:

(A) In general: The term 'tort maintenance coverage' means insurance coverage under which a person described in subparagraph (B), if involved in an accident with a person covered by personal protection insurance, retains a right to claim for injury based on fault for economic and noneconomic losses under applicable State law, without modification by any other provision of this Act.

(B) Tort maintenance insured: A person described in this subparagraph is a person covered by the form of insurance described in section 5(a)(2).

(C) Responsibility for payment: The responsibility for payment for any claim under subparagraph (A) is assumed by the insurer of the person with tort maintenance coverage to the extent of such coverage.

(21) Uncompensated economic loss:

(A) In general: The term 'uncompensated economic loss' means economic loss payable based on fault.

(B) Attorneys' fees: The term includes a reasonable attorney's fee calculated on the basis of the value of the attorney's efforts as reflected in payment to the attorney's client.

(C) Exclusions: The term does not include amounts paid under—

(i) personal protection insurance;

(ii) tort maintenance coverage;

(iii) no-fault or add-on motor vehicle insurance;

(iv) Federal, State, or private disability or sickness programs;

(v) Federal, State, or private health insurance programs;

(vi) employer wage continuation programs; or

(vii) workers' compensation or similar occupational compensation laws.

(22) Uninsured motorist: The term 'uninsured motorist' means the owner of a motor vehicle, including the resident relatives or dependents of the owner, who is uninsured undereither the personal protection system or the tort maintenance system described in section 5(a)—

(A) at the limits prescribed by the applicable State financial responsibility law; or

(B) an amount prescribed under section 5(b)(1)(A).

SECTION 5. AUTO CHOICE INSURANCE SYSTEM.

(a) Operation of the Right To Choose: Under this Act, a person shall have the right to choose between the following insurance systems:

(1) Personal protection system: A person may choose insurance under a system that provides for personal protection insurance for that person and any resident relative or dependent of that person.

(2) Tort maintenance system: A person may choose insurance under a system that provides for the form of motor vehicle insurance (including tort liability, no-fault, add-on, or uninsured motor vehicle insurance) that is otherwise required in the State in which the person is insured.

(b) Personal Protection System:

(1) Minimum policy requirements: In order for a personal protection insurance policy to be covered by this Act, a motor vehicle insurance policy issued by an insurer shall, at a minimum—

(A) provide personal protection insurance coverage—

(i) with no per accident limit; and

(ii) in coverage amounts equal to the greater of—

(I) the minimum per person limits of liability insurance for personal injury under the applicable State financial responsibility law; or

(II) in a State covered by a no-fault motor vehicle insurance law, the minimum level of insurance required for no-fault benefits;

(B) contain provisions for a waiver of certain tort rights in accordance with this Act; and

(C) contain provisions under the applicable State financial responsibility law relating to liability for—

(i) property damage; and

(ii) bodily injury to protect third parties whose rights to recover both economic and noneconomic loss are not affected by the immunities provided under this Act for those persons choosing personal protection insurance coverage.

(2) Superseding provision: This Act supersedes a State law to the extent that, with respect to the issuance of a personal protection insurance policy, the State law—

(A) would otherwise bar a provision that provides for the personal protection authorizations and accompanying immunities set forth in this Act; or

(B) is otherwise inconsistent with the requirements of this Act.

(3) Primacy of payment:

(A) In general: Personal protection insurance benefits shall be reduced by an amount equal to any benefits provided or required to be provided under an applicable Federal or State law for workers' compensation or any State-required nonoccupational disability insurance.

(B) Reimbursement of payors:

(i) In general: A personal protection insurer may take appropriate measures to ensure that any person otherwise eligible for personal protection benefits who has been paid or is being paid for losses payable by personal protection insurance from a source other than the applicable personal protection insurer shall not receive multiple payment for those losses.

(ii) Accrual of rights: Any right to payment for losses referred to in clause (i) from a personal protection insurer accrues only to that payor. Payments by a payor referred to in clause (i) shall not be counted against personal protection limits for personal protection insurance until such time as the payor is reimbursed under this subparagraph.

(4) Prompt and periodic payment:

(A) In general: A personal protection insurer may pay personal protection benefits periodically as losses accrue.

(B) Late payment: Unless the treatment or expenses related to the treatment are in reasonable dispute, a personal protection insurer who does not pay a claim for economic loss covered by a personal protection insurance policy issued under this Act within 30 days after payment is due, shall pay—

(i) the loss compounded at a rate of 24 percent per annum, as liquidated damages and in lieu of any penalty or exemplary damages; and

(ii) a reasonable attorney's fee calculated on the basis of the value of the attorney's efforts as reflected in payment to the attorney's client.

(C) Administration of personal protection benefits: To the extent consistent with this Act, any applicable provision of a State no-fault motor vehicle law or add-on law governing the administration of payment of benefits without reference to fault shall apply to the payment of benefits under personal protection insurance under this subsection.

(5) Motor vehicles with fewer than 4 load-bearing wheels: A personal protection insurer may offer, but shall not require, personal protection coverage of any motor vehicle that has fewer than 4 load-bearing wheels, not including the wheels of an attachment to the motor vehicle.

(6) Authorizations for personal protection insurers: A personal protection insurer may write personal protection coverage—

(A)(i) without any deductible; or

(ii) subject to a reasonable deductible, applicable in an amount not to exceed $1,000 per person per accident;

(B) with an exclusion of coverage for persons whose losses are caused by driving under the influence of alcohol or illegal drugs;

(C) at appropriately reduced premium rates, deductibles and exclusions reasonably related to health, disability, and accident coverage on an insured person; and

(D) the deductibles and exclusions described in subparagraphs (A) and (C) shall apply only to—

(i) the person named in the applicable insurance policy; and

(ii) the resident relatives or dependents of the person described in clause (i).

(c) Tort Maintenance System:

(1) Required tort maintenance coverage: The coverage for a person who chooses insurance under subsection (a)(2) shall include tort maintenance coverage at a level that is at least equivalent to the level of insurance required under the applicable State financial responsibility law for bodily injury liability.

(2) Administration of tort maintenance coverage benefits: To the extent consistent with this Act, any applicable provision of a State law governing the administration of payment of benefits under uninsured or underinsured motorist coverage applies to the payment of benefits under tort maintenance coverage under section 5(c).

(d) Effect of Choice on Resident Relatives and Dependents:

(1) In general: Except as provided in paragraph (2), a person who chooses either personal protection insurance or tort maintenance coverage also binds the resident relatives and dependents of that person.

(2) Exception: An adult resident relative or a dependent of a person described in paragraph (1) may select the form of insurance that that person does not select if the adult relative makes that selection expressly in writing.

(3) Implied consent: In any case in which the resident relative or dependent is injured in a motor vehicle accident, the coverage of such person shall be the same as the person described in paragraph (1).

(4) Terms and conditions: Insurers may specify reasonable terms and conditions governing the commencement, duration, and application of the chosen coverage depending on the number of motor vehicles and owners thereof in a household.

(e) Rules To Encourage Uniformity of Choice: In order to minimize conflict between the 2 options described in subsection (d), insurers may maintain and apply underwriting rules that encourage uniformity within a household.

(f) Failure To Elect Type of Insurance:

(1) In general: Any person who fails to elect a type of insurance under this section shall be deemed to have elected insurance under the tort maintenance system in effect in that State.

(2) Rule of construction: This subsection shall not be construed to prevent a State from enacting a law that deems a person who fails to elect a type of insurance under this section to have elected insurance under the personal protection system.

(g) Consumer Information Program: The State official charged with jurisdiction over insurance rates for motor vehicles shall establish and maintain a program designed to ensure that consumers are adequately informed about—

(1) the comparative cost of insurance under the personal protection system and the tort maintenance system; and

(2) the benefits, rights, and obligations of insurers and insureds under each system.

SECTION 6. SOURCE OF COMPENSATION IN CASES OF ACCIDENTAL INJURY.

(a) Accidents Involving Persons Choosing the Tort Maintenance System: A person described in section 5(a)(2) who is involved in an accident with another person shall be subject to applicable tort law for injury except that, based on fault, that person—

(1) may claim against any person covered by personal protection insurance only for uncompensated economic loss; and

(2) may be claimed against by a person covered by personal protection insurance only for uncompensated economic loss.

(b) Accidents Involving Persons With Personal Protection Insurance:

(1) Right to recover economic loss: A person covered by a personal protection insurance policy who is injured in an accident is compensated under that policy only for economic loss, without regard to fault.

(2) Right to sue for uncompensated economic loss based on fault: If a person who chooses personal protection insurance is—

(A) involved in an accident with a person insured under either the personal protection system or tort maintenance system under section 5(a); and

(B) sustains uncompensated economic loss, that person shall have the right to claim against the other person involved in the accident for that loss based on fault.

(c) Accidents Involving Persons With Personal Protection Insurance and Persons Who Are Unlawfully Uninsured:

(1) In general: A person covered by personal protection insurance who is involved in an accident with an uninsured motorist shall—

(A) be compensated under that insured person's insurance policy for economic loss without regard to fault; and

(B) have the right to claim against the uninsured motorist for economic loss and for noneconomic loss based on fault.

(2) Forfeiture of rights: An uninsured motorist forfeits the right to claim against a motorist who has chosen personal protection insurance for—

(A) noneconomic loss; and

(B) economic loss in an amount up to the amount of per-person bodily injury limits mandated by the applicable State financial responsibility law.

(d) Accidents Involving Motorists Under the Influence of Alcohol or Illegal Drugs or Engaging in Intentional Misconduct: A person who is insured under personal protection insurance shall have the right to claim, and be subject to a claim, for—

(1) driving under the influence of alcohol or illegal drugs (as those terms are defined under applicable State law); or

(2) intentional misconduct.

(e) Priority of Benefits: A person who is insured under the personal protection system or tort maintenance system under section 5(a) may only claim benefits under such coverage up to the limits selected by or on behalf of such person in the following priority:

(1) The coverage under which the injured person was an insured at the time of the accident.

(2) The coverage of a motor vehicle involved in the accident, if the person injured was an occupant of, or was struck as a pedestrian by, such

motor vehicle at the time of the accident, except that such person shall not recover under the coverage of both paragraph (1) and this paragraph.

(f) Subrogation Rights: A personal protection insurer is subrogated, to the extent of the obligations of that insurer, to all of the rights of the persons insured with personal protection insurance issued by the insurer with respect to an accident caused in whole or in part, as determined by applicable State law, by—

(1) the negligence of an uninsured motorist;

(2) operating a motor vehicle under the influence of alcohol or illegal drugs;

(3) intentional misconduct; or

(4) any other person who is not affected by the limitations on tort rights and liabilities under this Act.

(g) Rights of Lawfully Uninsured Persons: Nothing in this Act shall be construed to affect the tort rights of any person lawfully uninsured under the terms of an applicable State law for insurance under either the personal protection system or tort maintenance system under section 5(a).

(h) Rights of Persons Occupying Motor Vehicles With Fewer Than 4 Load-Bearing Wheels: Nothing in this Act shall be construed to affect the tort rights of a person who occupies a motor vehicle with fewer than 4 load-bearing wheels or an attachment thereto, unless an applicable contract for personal protection insurance under which that person is insured specifies otherwise. The preceding sentence applies without regard to whether the person is otherwise legally insured for personal protection insurance or tort maintenance coverage.

(i) Renewal or Cancellation: An insurer shall not cancel, fail to renew, or increase the premium of a person insured by the insurer solely because that insured person or any other injured person made a claim—

(1) for personal protection insurance benefits; or

(2) if there is no basis for ascribing fault to the insured or one for whom the insured is vicariously liable, for tort maintenance coverage.

(j) Immunity: Unless an insurer or an insurance agent willfully misrepresents the available choices or fraudulently induces the election of one motor vehicle insurance system described in paragraph (1) over the other, no insurer or insurance agent, employee of such insurer or agent, insurance producer representing a motor vehicle insurer, automobile residual market plan, or attorney licensed to practice law within a State, shall be liable in an action for damages on account of—

(1) an election of—

(A) the tort maintenance system under section 5(a); or

(B) the personal protection system under section 5(a); or

(2) a failure to make a required election.

SECTION 7. RULES OF CONSTRUCTION.

Nothing in this Act shall be construed—

(1) to waive or affect any defense of sovereign immunity asserted by any State under any law or by the United States;

(2) to affect the awarding of punitive damages under any State law;

(3) to preempt State choice-of-law rules with respect to claims brought by a foreign nation or a citizen of a foreign nation;

(4) to affect the right of any court to transfer venue, to apply the law of a foreign nation, or to dismiss a claim of a foreign nation or of a citizen of a foreign nation on the ground of inconvenient forum;

(5) subject to paragraph (1), to create or vest jurisdiction in the district courts of the United States over any motor vehicle accident liability or damages action subject to this Act which is not otherwise properly in the United States District Court;

(6) to prevent insurers and insureds from contracting to limit recovery for lost wages and income under personal protection coverage in such manner that only 60 percent or more of lost wages or income is covered;

(7) to prevent an insurer from contracting with personal protection insureds, as permitted by applicable State law, to have submitted to arbitration any dispute with respect to payment of personal protection benefits;

(8) to relieve a motorist of the obligations imposed by applicable State law to purchase tort liability insurance for bodily injury to protect third parties who are not affected by the immunities under this Act;

(9) to preclude a State from enacting, for all motor vehicle accident cases including cases covered by this Act, a minimum dollar value for defined classes of cases involving death or serious bodily injury;

(10) to preclude a State from providing that forms of insurance other than those listed in section 5(b)(3) shall be subtracted from personal protection insurance benefits otherwise payable for injury;

(11) to preclude a State from enacting a law that—

(A) allows litigation by tort maintenance insureds against personal protection insureds for economic and noneconomic loss; and

(B) assures through a reallocation device that the advantage of tort claim waivers by personal protection insureds against tort maintenance insureds is reflected in the premiums of personal protection insureds; or

(12) to alter or diminish the authority or obligation of the Federal courts to construe the terms of this Act.

SECTION 8. APPLICABILITY TO STATES; CHOICE OF LAW; AND JURISDICTION.

(a) Election of Nonapplicability by States: This Act shall not apply with respect to a State if such State enacts a statute that—

(1) cites the authority of this subsection;

(2) declares the election of such State that this Act shall not apply; and

(3) contains no other provision.

(b) Nonapplicability Based on State Finding:

(1) In general: This Act shall not apply with respect to a State, if—

(A) the State official charged with jurisdiction over insurance rates for motor vehicles makes a finding that the statewide average motor vehicle premiums for bodily injury insurance in effect immediately before the effective date of this Act will not be reduced by an average of at least 30 percent for persons choosing personal protection insurance (without including in the calculation for personal protection insureds any cost for uninsured, underinsured, or medical payments coverages);

(B) a finding described under subparagraph (A) is supported by evidence adduced in a public hearing and reviewable under the applicable State administrative procedure law; and

(C) a finding described under subparagraph (A) and any review of such finding under subparagraph (B) occurs not later than 90 days after the date of enactment of this Act. (2) Comparison of bodily injury premiums: For purposes of making a comparison under paragraph (1)(A) of premiums for personal protection insurance with preexisting premiums for bodily injury insurance (in effect immediately before the date of enactment of this Act), the preexisting bodily injury insurance premiums shall include premiums for—

(A) bodily injury liability, uninsured and underinsured motorists' liability, and medical payments coverage; and

(B) if applicable, no-fault benefits under a no-fault motor vehicle law or add-on law.

(c) Choice of Law: In disputes between citizens of States that elect nonapplicability under subsection (a) and citizens of States that do not make such an election, ordinary choice of law principles shall apply.

(d) Jurisdiction: This Act shall not confer jurisdiction on the district courts of the United States under section 1331 or 1337 of title 28, United States Code.

(e) Statutes of Limitations: Nothing in this Act shall supersede an applicable State law that imposes a statute of limitations for claims related to an injury caused by an accident, except that such statute shall be tolled during the period wherein any personal protection or tort maintenance benefits are paid.

SECTION 9. EFFECTIVE DATE.

This Act shall take effect 90 days after the date of enactment of this Act.

APPENDIX 15:

DIRECTORY OF STATE WORKERS' COMPENSATION BOARDS

STATE	DEPARTMENT	ADDRESS	TELEPHONE
ALABAMA	Workers' Compensation Division, Department of Industrial Relations	Industrial Relations Building, Montgomery, AL 36131	(334) 242-2868
ALASKA	Workers' Compensation Division, Department of Labor	1111 West 8th Street, Suite 307, P.O. Box 25512, Juneau, AK 99802-5512	(907) 465-2790
ARIZONA	Industrial Commission	800 West Washington Street, P. O. Box 19070, Phoenix, AZ 85005-9070	(602) 542-4411
ARKANSAS	Workers' Compensation Commission	4th and Spring Streets, P. O. Box 950, Little Rock, AR 72203-9050	(501) 682-3930
CALIFORNIA	Division of Workers' Compensation	45 Fremont Street, Suite 3160, P. O. Box 420603, San Francisco, CA 94142	(415) 975-0700
COLORADO	Division of Workers' Compensation	1515 Arapahoe Street, Denver, CO 80202	(303) 575-8700
CONNECTICUT	Workers' Compensation Commission	21 Oak Street, Hartford, CT 06106	(860) 493-1500
DELAWARE	Industrial Accident Board	4425 N. Market Street, 3rd Floor, Wilmington, DE 19802	(302) 761-8200
DISTRICT OF COLUMBIA	Office of Workers' Compensation	1200 Upshur St. NW, 2nd Floor, Washington, DC 20011	(202) 576-6265
FLORIDA	Division of Workers' Compensation	301 Forrest Building, 2728 Centerview Drive, Tallahassee, FL 32399-0680	(904) 488-2514
GEORGIA	Board of Workers' Compensation	270 Peachtree Street NW Atlanta, GA 30303-1205	(404) 656-3875

STATE	DEPARTMENT	ADDRESS	TELEPHONE
HAWAII	Disability Compensation Division, Department of Labor and Industrial Relations	830 Punchbowl Street, Room 211, P. O. Box 3769, Honolulu, HI 96812	(808) 586-9151
IDAHO	Industrial Commission	Statehouse Mail, 317 Main Street, P. O. Box 83720, Boise, ID 83720-0041	(208) 334-6000
ILLINOIS	Industrial Commission	100 West Randolph Street, Suite 8-200, Chicago, IL 60601	(312) 814-6500
INDIANA	Workers' Compensation Board	402 West Washington Street, Room W-196, Indianapolis, IN 46204	(317) 232-3808
IOWA	Division of Industrial Services, Iowa Workforce Development	1000 East Grand Avenue, Des Moines, IA 50319	(515) 281-5934
KANSAS	Division of Workers' Compensation, Department of Human Resources	800 SW Jackson Street, Suite 600, Topeka, KS 66612-1227	(913) 296-3441
KENTUCKY	Department of Workers Claims	1270 Louisville Road, Perimeter Park West, Bldg. C, Frankfort, KY 40601	(502) 564-5550
LOUISIANA	Office of Workers' Compensation	1001 North 23rd Street, P. O. Box 94040, Baton Rouge, LA 70802-9040	(504) 342-7555
MAINE	Workers' Compensation Board	27 State House Station, Augusta, ME 04333	(207) 287-3751
MARYLAND	Workers' Compensation Commission	6 North Liberty Street, Baltimore, MD 21201-3785	(410) 767-0900
MASSACHU-SETTS	Dept. of Industrial Accidents	600 Washington Street, 7th Floor, Boston, MA 02111	(617) 727-4900

STATE	DEPARTMENT	ADDRESS	TELEPHONE
MICHIGAN	Bureau of Workers' Disability Compensation	201 North Washington Square, P. O. Box 30016, Lansing, MI 48909	(517) 322-1296
MINNESOTA	Division of Workers' Compensation, Department of Labor and Industry	443 Lafayette Road North, St. Paul, MN 55155-4319	(612) 296-6490
MISSISSIPPI	Workers' Compensation Commission	1428 Lakeland Drive, P. O. Box 5300, Jackson, MS 39296-5300	(601) 987-4200
MISSOURI	Division of Workers' Compensation, Department of Labor and Industrial Relations	P. O. Box 58, Jefferson City, MO 65102	(573) 751-4231
MONTANA	Employment Relations Division, Department of Labor and Industry	1805 Prospect Avenue, P. O. Box 8011, Helena, MT 59604-8011	(406) 444-6530
NEBRASKA	Workers' Compensation Court	Capitol Building, P. O. Box 98908, Lincoln, NE 68509-8908	(402) 471-2568
NEVADA	State Industrial Insurance System	515 East Musser Street, Carson City, NV 89714	(702) 687-5220
NEW HAMPSHIRE	Workers' Compensation Division, Department of Labor	95 Pleasant Street, Concord, NH 03301	(603) 271-3176
NEW JERSEY	Division of Workers' Compensation, Department of Labor	C. N. 381, Trenton, NJ 08625-0381	(609) 292-2414
NEW MEXICO	Workers' Compensation Administration	2410 Centre Drive SE, P. O. Box 27198, Albuquerque, NM 87125-7198	(505) 841-6000
NEW YORK	Workers' Compensation Board	100 Broadway-Menands, Albany NY 12241	(518) 474-6670
NORTH CAROLINA	Industrial Commission	Dobbs Building, 430 North Salisbury Street, Raleigh, NC 27611	(919) 733-4820

STATE	DEPARTMENT	ADDRESS	TELEPHONE
NORTH DAKOTA	Workers' Compensation Bureau	500 East Front Avenue, Bismarck, ND 58504-5685	(701) 328-3800
OHIO	Bureau of Workers' Compensation	30 West Spring Street, Columbus, OH 43266-0581	(614) 466-8751
OKLAHOMA	Workers' Compensation Court	1915 North Stiles Avenue, Oklahoma City, OK 73105-4904	(405) 557-7600
OREGON	Workers' Compensation Division	350 Winter Street NE, Salem, OR 97310	(503) 945-7881
PENNSYLVANIA	Bureau of Workers' Compensation, Department of Labor and Industry	1171 So. Cameron Street, Rm. 103, Harrisburg, PA 17104-2501	(717) 783-5421
RHODE ISLAND	Division of Workers' Compensation	Department of Labor, 610 Manton Avenue, P.O. Box 3500, Providence, RI 02909	(401) 457-1800
SOUTH CAROLINA	Workers' Compensation Commission	1612 Marion Street, P. O. Box 1715, Columbia, SC 29202-1715	(803) 737-5700
SOUTH DAKOTA	Division of Labor & Management, Department of Labor	700 Governors Dr., Kneip Bldg., Pierre, SD 57501-2291	(605) 773-3681
TENNESSEE	Division of Workers' Compensation, Department of Labor	Gateway Plaza, 2nd Floor, 710 James Robertson Parkway, Nashville,. TN 37243-0661	(615) 741-2395
TEXAS	Workers' Compensation Commission	Southfield Building, 4000 South IH-35, Austin, TX 78704-7491	(512) 448-7900
UTAH	Industrial Accident Division, Industrial Commission	160 East 300 South, 3rd Floor, P. O. Box 146610, Salt Lake City, UT 84114-6610	(801) 530-6800

STATE	DEPARTMENT	ADDRESS	TELEPHONE
VERMONT	Department of Labor and Industry	National Life Building, Drawer 20, Montpelier, VT 05620-3401	(802) 828-2286
VIRGINIA	Workers' Compensation Commission	1000 DMV Drive, Richmond, VA 23220	(804) 367-8600
WASHINGTON	Department of Labor and Industries	7273 Linderson Way SW, Tumwater	(360) 902-5800
WEST VIRGINIA	Workers' Compensation Division	4700 MacCorkle Avenue SE, Charleston, WV 25304	(304) 926-5048
WISCONSIN	Workers' Compensation Division, Department of Workforce Development	201 East Washington Avenue, P. O. Box 7901, Madison, WI 53707	(608) 266-1340
WYOMING	Workers' Compensation Division	122 West 25th Street, 2nd Floor, Herschler Building, East Wing, Cheyenne, WY 82002-0700	(307) 777-7159

GLOSSARY

GLOSSARY

Act of God - Manifestation of the forces of nature which are unpredictable and difficult to anticipate, such as lightning and earthquakes.

Actual Cash Value - The value of property as figured by determining what it would cost to replace the property, and then adjusting this replacement cost by subtracting an amount that reflects depreciation.

Actuary - One who computes various insurance and property costs, and calculates the cost of life insurance risks and insurance premiums.

Agency - The relationship between a principal and an agent who is employed by the principal, to perform certain acts dealing with third parties.

Agent - One who represents another known as the principal.

American Arbitration Association (AAA) - National organization of arbitrators from whose panel arbitrators are selected for labor and civil disputes.

Annuitant - The person entitled to receive annuity payments.

Annuity - The right to receive fixed, periodic payments over a specified term.

Beneficiary - A person who is designated to receive property upon the death of another, such as the beneficiary of a life insurance policy, who receives the proceeds upon the death of the insured.

Collision Insurance - An element of car insurance that pays the insured for damages, above the policy's deductible, sustained by the insured vehicle resulting from a collision with another vehicle or object.

Comprehensive Insurance Coverage - An element of car insurance that pays the insured for damages to the insured's vehicle caused by anything other than a collision, including vandalism, fire, theft and natural disasters.

Contract - A contract is an agreement between two or more persons which creates an obligation to do or not to do a particular thing.

Covenant - A covenant is an agreement or promise to do or not to do a particular thing, as to bind oneself in contract.

Decedent - A deceased person.

Deductible - An amount an insured person must pay before they are entitled to recover money from the insurer, in connection with a loss or expense covered by an insurance policy.

Fiduciary - A fiduciary is a person having a legal duty, created by an undertaking, to act primarily for the benefit of another in matters connected with the undertaking.

Fraud - A false representation of a matter of fact, whether by words or by conduct, by false or misleading allegations, or by concealment of that which should have been disclosed, which deceives and is intended to deceive another, and thereby causes injury to that person.

Guardian - A person who is entrusted with the management of the property and/or person of another who is incapable, due to age or incapacity, to administer their own affairs.

Heirs - Those individuals who, by law, inherit an estate of an ancestor who dies without a will.

Indemnification Clause - An indemnification clause in a contract refers to the agreement by one party to secure the other party against loss or damage which may occur in the future in connection with performance of the contract.

Indemnify - To hold another harmless for loss or damage which has already occurred, or which may occur in the future.

Inherit - To take as an heir at law by descent rather than by will.

Inheritance - Property inherited by heirs according to the laws of descent and distribution.

Insurance - A contingency agreement, supported by consideration, whereby the insured receives a benefit, e.g. money, in the event the contingency occurs.

Liability - Refers to one's obligation to do or refrain from doing something, such as the payment of a debt.

Liability Insurance Coverage - Refers to compensation paid to third parties who are injured or whose property is damaged due to the fault of the insured.

Life Expectancy - The period of time which a person is statistically expected to live, based on such factors as their present age and sex.

Life Insurance - A contract between an insured and an insurer whereby the insurer promises to pay a sum of money upon the death of the insured to his or her designated beneficiary, in return for the periodic payment of money, known as a premium.

Loss Damage Waiver (LDW) - Rental car insurance, also known as collision damage waiver, that makes the rental car company responsible for damage to, or theft of, a rental car.

Medicare - The program governed by the Social Security Administration to provide medical and hospital coverage to the aged or disabled.

No-Fault Automobile Insurance - Refers to laws governing automobile insurance that require the insurance companies of each person in an accident to pay for medical bills and lost wages of their insured, up to a certain amount, regardless of who was at fault.

Pension Benefit Guaranty Corporation (PBGC) - A public, nonprofit insurance fund that provides some limited coverage against bankrupt pension funds.

Premium - The periodic payment of money by an insured to an insurer for insurance protection against specified losses.

Private mortgage insurance (PMI) - Insurance generally required of homeowners who put less than a 20% downpayment on their home purchase, in order to reimburse the mortgage lender if the buyer defaults on the loan and the foreclosure sale price is less than the amount owed the lender.

Subrogation - In insurance law, the process which occurs when an insurance company that has paid on an insurance claim "stands in the shoes" of the claimant and takes legal action against any third parties who were responsible for the claimant's damages.

Underwrite - In insurance law, it refers to the assumption of the risk of loss to the insured's person or property, by the insurer of the insurance policy.

Underwriter - Another term for an insurer, one who assumes the risk of another's loss and compensates for the loss under the terms of an insurance policy.

Unemployment Insurance - A program run jointly by federal and state governments that provides money benefits for a specified time to an employee who has been laid off or terminated from a job.

Uninsured motorist coverage - An element of car insurance that compensates the insured for injuries resulting from an accident with an uninsured motorist or a hit-and-run driver.

BIBLIOGRAPHY

BIBLIOGRAPHY

A Guide To Long-Term Care Insurance. Washington, DC: American Association of Retired Persons, 1991.

Black's Law Dictionary, Fifth Edition. St. Paul, MN: West Publishing Company, 1979.

Burton, Jr., John F. *Workers' Compensation Deskbook*. Horsham, PA: LRP Publications, 1992.

Insurance News Network (Date Visited: September 1998), http://www.insure.com/.

Joost, Robert H. *Automobile Insurance and No-Fault Law* 2d. New York, NY: Clark Boardman Callaghan, 1995.

Leitner, David L.*Recurring Issues in Insurance Disputes*. Chicago, IL: American Bar Association Tort and Insurance Practice Section, 1996.

Monthly Vital Statistics Report, Life Expectancy Tables. U.S. Department of Health (Date Visited: September 1998), http://www.cdc.gov/nchs/.

New York Lawyers Diary and Manual. Newark, NJ: Skinder-Strauss Associates, 1996.

Understanding COBRA Benefits. U.S. Department of Labor Pension and Welfare Benefits Administration (PWBA) (Date Visited: September 1998), http://www.dol.gov/dol/pwba/.

Understanding Social Security. U.S. Department of Health and Human Services, Social Security Administration, 1992.